Urban Sprawl

Other Books in the Current Controversies Series

Biodiversity

Blogs

Capital Punishment

Developing Nations

Domestic Wiretaping

Drug Trafficking

Espionage and Intelligence

Food

Global Warming

Homosexuality

Illegal Immigration

Online Social Networking

Pollution

Prescription Drugs

Rap Music and Culture

School Violence

The Middle East

The Wage Gap

Violence Against Women

Urban Sprawl

Debra A. Miller, Book Editor

GREENHAVEN PRESS
A part of Gale, Cengage Learning

GALE
CENGAGE Learning

Detroit • New York • San Francisco • New Haven, Conn • Waterville, Maine • London

Christine Nasso, *Publisher*
Elizabeth Des Chenes, *Managing Editor*

For more information, contact:
Greenhaven Press
27500 Drake Rd.
Farmington Hills, MI 48331-3535
Or you can visit our Internet site at gale.cengage.com

LIBRARY OF CONGRESS CATALOGING-IN-PUBLICATION DATA

Urban sprawl / Debra A. Miller, book editor.
    p. cm. -- (Current controversies)
    Includes bibliographical references and index.
    ISBN-13: 978-0-7377-3966-4 (hardcover)
    ISBN-13: 978-0-7377-3967-1 (pbk.)
    1. Cities and towns--Growth. 2. Land use, Rural. 3. Land use, Urban. I. Miller, Debra A.
    HT371.U73 2008
    307.76--dc22
                                                            2008001003

Printed in the United States of America
    1 2 3 4 5   12 11 10 09 08

ED230

Contents

Foreword   13

Introduction   16

Chapter 1: Is Urban Sprawl a Serious Problem?

Chapter Overview   21

Environmental Literacy Council

Rising prosperity and affordable transportation in recent
decades has caused a migration of inner city residents to
outer, less densely populated areas; this expansion, called
urban sprawl, is part of a search for safer neighborhoods,
better schools, and affordable housing, but it also has
negative effects.

Yes: Urban Sprawl Is a Serious Problem

Urban Sprawl Causes a Host of Problems for   25
U.S. Communities

Don DeGraaf, Jill Lankford, and Sam Lankford

The sprawling development pattern around U.S. cities
has caused problems for inner cities, such as a loss of
public communal space, decreased social ties, overdepen-
dence on automobiles, environmental deterioration, and
health issues.

Urban Sprawl Destroys Habitat and   33
Farmland and Harms Biodiversity

Cynthia Berlin

Urban sprawl also is a problem for smaller U.S. cities because it destroys natural habitat that is essential to biodiversity, causes an alarming loss of farmland, and increases
costs for roads and other infrastructure.

Urban Sprawl Is Partially to Blame for   39
the Nation's Obesity Problem

Brian Johnson

Low-density development associated with sprawl is partially to blame for rising levels of obesity in the United
States because people in such developments lead a more
sedentary, automobile-dependent lifestyle.

Urban Sprawl Also Afflicts   43
Developing Countries
　　Neha Menon

　　Developing countries are also beginning to experience
　　problems with urban sprawl because as they urbanize,
　　most developing countries are following the unsustain-
　　able Western development model.

No: Urban Sprawl Is Not a Serious Problem

Urban Sprawl Is the American Dream   49
　　Rachel Dicarlo

　　Urban sprawl is the logical result of a city's growth as it
　　matures economically, and the suburbs have made it pos-
　　sible for ordinary Americans to enjoy the privacy, space,
　　leisure time, and choice that were once available only to
　　the rich.

Many Suburbs Are Neighborhoods that   55
Provide Good Places to Live
　　Terry O'Neill

　　Many suburban areas are actually good places to live,
　　providing consumers with two-car garages, backyard
　　spaces for children, and just enough privacy combined
　　with sufficient density to foster neighborly friendships
　　and other social associations.

Concerns About Urban Sprawl   59
Are Class-Based Objections
to Middle-Class Developments
　　Robert Bruegmann

　　The suburbs provide the privacy, mobility, freedom, and
　　jobs expected by ordinary urban residents, and criticisms
　　of urban sprawl are generally class-based objections to
　　middle-class tastes motivated by self-interest and resis-
　　tance to change.

Some Criticisms of Urban Sprawl Are 68
Not Supported by Serious Research
Samuel R. Staley and Matthew Hisrich

Researchers agree that urban sprawl increases automobile usage and reduces the amount of agricultural land; however, sprawl reduces traffic congestion, provides greater mobility, and research is unclear on other claims of sprawl costs.

Chapter 2: Does Urban Sprawl Harm the Environment?

Chapter Preface 73

Yes: Urban Sprawl Harms the Environment

Urban Sprawl Is a Major 76
Environmental Concern
Clean Water Action Council

Urban sprawl is chewing up farmland, destroying wildlife habitat, causing air and water pollution, increasing energy consumption, reducing scenic qualities and tourism attractions, and causing a number of other problems for the United States.

There Is a Clear Connection Between Urban 82
Sprawl and Air Pollution
Matt Weiser

Cities such as Bakersfield, California, are beginning to realize that urban sprawl makes smog and air pollution worse by concentrating growth at the edges of cities, forcing people to drive farther to reach work and shopping, putting more cars on the road, and limiting opportunities for walking, biking, and public transit.

Urban Sprawl Threatens the Nation's 90
Water Supplies
Brian Johnson

Urban development may be worsening the nation's water supply problems because replacing natural ground with paved surfaces reduces the amount of rainwater absorbed into the earth as groundwaters that replenish aquifers and other water resources, and instead sends it into streams and rivers as polluted runoff.

Urban Sprawl Is Threatening Some   94
of the Most Endangered Wildlife
    Eddie Nickens

    Ever-expanding suburbs are gobbling up millions of acres
    of wildlife habitat every year, destroying the habitat of
    many animal species listed as threatened or endangered
    by the federal government.

Urban Sprawl Is Contributing to   102
Global Warming
    Worldwatch Institute

    Sprawling urban areas in the United States are helping to
    make road transportation the fastest growing source of
    carbon emissions that are warming the earth's atmo-
    sphere, and if developing countries follow the U.S. lead,
    the problem could get much worse.

**No: Urban Sprawl Does Not Harm
the Environment**

Urban Sprawl and Automobiles Cause   105
Fewer Environmental Problems than Many
People Think
    Ted Balaker and Sam Staley

    Suburban sprawl and automobiles have gained a reputa-
    tion as scourges of modern U.S. society, but in reality, air
    quality is improving, very little open space has been
    paved over, and driving less will probably not solve glo-
    bal warming.

There Is No Crisis over Disappearing   112
Farmland or Open Space
    Owen Courrèges

    There is no need to protect farmland in the United States
    because the demand for farmland has decreased dramati-
    cally over recent decades due to the success of high-yield
    agriculture, and protecting privately owned farms will
    not provide wildlife habitat or public recreational ben-
    efits.

Urban Sprawl in Some Cases   **115**
Can Help Farmers

 Wayne Wenzel

 Farmers are supposed to hate urban sprawl, but urban
 development sometimes can increase the value of prime
 farmland from six to fifteen times the value of agricultural land, allowing farmers to trade their farms for more
 acres of prime farmland further from the city.

Urban Sprawl May Not Be So Bad   **118**
for Wildlife

 Space Daily

 Recent studies of the diversity of bird populations in urban sprawl and natural forest areas of Tennessee found
 that, in some cases, urban areas had more diversity than
 did the native forests, suggesting that urban sprawl is not
 always bad for wildlife.

Chapter 3: Does Urban Sprawl Contribute to the Decline of Cities?

Chapter Preface   **121**

Yes: Urban Sprawl Contributes to the Decline of Cities

Urban Sprawl Has Impoverished U.S. Cities **124**

 Olga Bonfiglio

 Urban sprawl is an injustice that has caused U.S. cities to
 decline into places of poverty, abandoned buildings, run-
 down neighborhoods, poor schools, pot-holed roads,
 polluted waterways, and feelings of alienation and disconnection among residents.

Bigger, Older Cities Continue to   **132**
Lose Populations

 Associated Press

 America's largest cities are losing ground, as Americans
 continue to move away from cities to much smaller, suburban communities where housing is cheaper and schools
 are better.

Inner Cities Continue to   135
Decline Economically
   Daniel Muniz
   About half of the nation's largest cities have lost jobs due
   to the lack of business investment because the suburbs
   are often more welcoming of economic development.

**No: Urban Sprawl Does Not Contribute
to the Decline of Cities**

Urban Sprawl Is an Inherent Part   139
of Urbanization
   Witold Rybczynski
   Sprawl is a universal and long-standing feature of urban
   development worldwide and is driven by the decisions of
   millions of individuals to live in single-family houses on
   a parcel of privately owned land.

Urban Sprawl Has Kept Housing Prices   144
Affordable in Cities that Have Not Tried to
Restrict Suburban Growth
   Wendell Cox
   Cities such as Montreal, Canada, which have resisted
   overly restrictive land use policies designed to restrict ur-
   ban sprawl, have been able to keep housing prices afford-
   able and at historical norms in relation to incomes.

Chapter 4: Should Urban Sprawl Be Restricted?

Chapter Preface   149

Yes: Urban Sprawl Should Be Restricted

Smart Growth Developments Are Effective   152
and Becoming Commonplace in U.S. Cities
   Mark Alden Branch
   Mixed-use smart growth developments, such as developments anchored to rail lines and high-density developments created by government growth boundaries, are
   successful, popular among Americans, and increasingly
   common in U.S. cities.

The City of Portland, Oregon,   **156**
Provides an Example of Successful
Smart Growth Policies

Mass Market Retailers

The strong smart-growth planning controls adopted by
Portland, Oregon, in the 1970s have protected the city
from urban sprawl and created a livable city, surrounded
by farmland with less traffic and more efficient public
transportation than many other metropolitan areas.

Smart Growth Solutions Are Better at   **159**
Slowing Urban Sprawl than Population
Control Strategies

Sierra Club

Smart growth solutions that channel growth into areas
with existing infrastructure are effective at slowing
sprawling urban growth; however, solutions that focus on
curtailing population growth by increasing density increase the amount of sprawl.

Smart Growth Works Best when Directed   **168**
Away from Ecologically Sensitive Areas

Defenders of Wildlife

Smart growth concentrates on developing the urban core
and developing it in dense patterns in order to protect
fish and wildlife habitat, but development must avoid
ecologically sensitive areas in order for biodiversity to
thrive.

No: Urban Sprawl Should Not Be Restricted

Smart Growth Is a Threat to the   **172**
American Dream

Wendell Cox

The smart growth movement would raise housing prices,
increase traffic congestion, reduce the number of accessible jobs, and add to air pollution, and these effects
would threaten the American dream of home ownership,
employment, and prosperity.

The Smart Growth/New Urbanism   177
Policies Have Many Problems, Even in
Portland, Oregon
    Kennedy Smith

    The smart growth policies of the New Urbanism move-
    ment is still more theory than practice, and even the de-
    velopment projects in Portland, Oregon, have problems
    such as financing for parking, mass transport, and other
    infrastructure.

Population Control Is Essential to   180
Stopping Urban Sprawl
    NumbersUSA

    High-density, smart-growth development is not the an-
    swer to urban sprawl because more people always pro-
    duce a larger ecological footprint; the only way to solve
    sprawl in the long run is to address the problem of over-
    population.

Organizations to Contact   186

Bibliography   189

Index   194

Foreword

By definition, controversies are "discussions of questions in which opposing opinions clash" (Webster's Twentieth Century Dictionary Unabridged). Few would deny that controversies are a pervasive part of the human condition and exist on virtually every level of human enterprise. Controversies transpire between individuals and among groups, within nations and between nations. Controversies supply the grist necessary for progress by providing challenges and challengers to the status quo. They also create atmospheres where strife and warfare can flourish. A world without controversies would be a peaceful world; but it also would be, by and large, static and prosaic.

The Series' Purpose

The purpose of the *Current Controversies* series is to explore many of the social, political, and economic controversies dominating the national and international scenes today. Titles selected for inclusion in the series are highly focused and specific. For example, from the larger category of criminal justice, *Current Controversies* deals with specific topics such as police brutality, gun control, white collar crime, and others. The debates in *Current Controversies* also are presented in a useful, timeless fashion. Articles and book excerpts included in each title are selected if they contribute valuable, long-range ideas to the overall debate. And wherever possible, current information is enhanced with historical documents and other relevant materials. Thus, while individual titles are current in focus, every effort is made to ensure that they will not become quickly outdated. Books in the *Current Controversies* series will remain important resources for librarians, teachers, and students for many years.

In addition to keeping the titles focused and specific, great care is taken in the editorial format of each book in the series. Book introductions and chapter prefaces are offered to provide background material for readers. Chapters are organized around several key questions that are answered with diverse opinions representing all points on the political spectrum. Materials in each chapter include opinions in which authors clearly disagree as well as alternative opinions in which authors may agree on a broader issue but disagree on the possible solutions. In this way, the content of each volume in *Current Controversies* mirrors the mosaic of opinions encountered in society. Readers will quickly realize that there are many viable answers to these complex issues. By questioning each author's conclusions, students and casual readers can begin to develop the critical thinking skills so important to evaluating opinionated material.

Current Controversies is also ideal for controlled research. Each anthology in the series is composed of primary sources taken from a wide gamut of informational categories including periodicals, newspapers, books, U.S. and foreign government documents, and the publications of private and public organizations. Readers will find factual support for reports, debates, and research papers covering all areas of important issues. In addition, an annotated table of contents, an index, a book and periodical bibliography, and a list of organizations to contact are included in each book to expedite further research.

Perhaps more than ever before in history, people are confronted with diverse and contradictory information. During the Persian Gulf War, for example, the public was not only treated to minute-to-minute coverage of the war, it was also inundated with critiques of the coverage and countless analyses of the factors motivating U.S. involvement. Being able to sort through the plethora of opinions accompanying today's major issues, and to draw one's own conclusions, can be a complicated and frustrating struggle. It is the editors' hope that *Current Controversies* will help readers with this struggle.

Introduction

"In the United States, sprawl is closely linked with the romanticized American dream of owning a home in the country, far away from the hustle and bustle of city life."

Urban sprawl is the name given to the unplanned expansion of urban development into rural areas surrounding cities. For many decades, sprawl has been a fact of modern life, not only in the United States but also in other wealthy, developed countries. Today, even cities in some developing countries are beginning to experience similar rapid growth. The causes of this phenomenon are varied, but three major contributing factors appear to be: growing human populations, increasing economic prosperity, and improvements in transportation that allow people to live farther from where they work.

In the United States, sprawl is closely linked with the romanticized American dream of owning a home in the country, far away from the hustle and bustle of city life. During the early years of the nation's existence, while some Americans lived and worked in small towns, the large majority lived in rural areas on farms or large ranches in the western frontier. The increased productivity and economic gains resulting from the industrial revolution beginning in the late 1700s, however, created new jobs in the cities and attracted rural residents, as well as hundreds of thousands of immigrants, to U.S. cities. The rapid rise in U.S. urban populations brought new problems, such as overcrowded housing conditions, poor sanitation, and epidemics. In addition, the reliance on coal as an energy source produced choking fumes that polluted city air and made it increasingly unhealthy.

During the early 20th century, these poor living conditions in the nation's large cities prompted some wealthier and upper-middle-class residents to purchase homes in the countryside, amid farms and forested areas. This push outward from the cities was aided by changes in transportation, first the invention of the trolley car and railroads, and then the automobile, which allowed people living in outlying areas to travel easily to jobs in the city. Other factors that encouraged urban expansion included the introduction of low-cost construction methods and the affordability of rural land.

The end of World War II and the availability of cheap oil triggered an economic boom during the 1950s and 1960s that permitted less wealthy American workers—many of them World War II veterans eager to start their families and civilian lives—to buy automobiles and realize the dream of home ownership that once was reserved for the rich. At the same time, federal spending on an interstate highway program made outlying areas more accessible, and federal loans helped to finance developments in these areas. The suburbs soon became the hoped-for destination for many U.S. workers and a growing American middle class.

One of the earliest and most famous of these post–World War II suburban communities was Levittown, New York. In fact, Levittown—a planned community built on farmland outside New York City between 1947 and 1951—became a model on which many suburban communities across the country were based. Levittown was named after its builder, the firm of Levitt & Sons, Inc., a construction firm that won a Navy contract to build homes for shipyard workers in Norfolk, Virginia, during World War II. This work helped the firm develop mass-production building techniques that allowed it to quickly build large numbers of homes.

With this experience, the company was able to capitalize on a housing boom at war's end. Material shortages meant that few houses were built during the war and 16 million returning U.S. servicemen created a heightened need for millions of new homes. After years of life-threatening military service, many veterans longed for the chance to marry, raise a family, and live a peaceful life. Levitt & Sons recognized this need for postwar housing and announced plans to build 2,000 simple, inexpensive homes on nearby farmland. The plan was enhanced by the availability of a new federal program that helped returning servicemen qualify for low-interest, insured "GI Loans" to finance their new homes.

The firm was able to build the Levittown homes cheaply and fast not only because the rural land was inexpensive, but also thanks to several construction innovations. First, the houses were built without basements on concrete slabs. In addition, the lumber was precut and shipped by rail from a lumberyard the firm owned in California. Nails also came from a firm-owned factory. Finally, nonunion contractors were used and houses were constructed all at the same time in a production manner.

These techniques were highly successful and the Levitt homes became more popular than anyone could have imagined. The first homes were immediately occupied and demand was so great that the firm quickly built 4,000 more. Later, the firm built larger, ranch-style homes using the same formula, and ultimately the Levittown community grew to more than 17,000 homes and included its own schools, shopping centers, post office, and community center. The Levitts later built similar planned communities in Pennsylvania, New Jersey, and Puerto Rico.

Levittown's popularity and success made it a symbol for suburban living in the United States. In July 1950, William Levitt, one of the firm's principals, was featured on the cover of *Time* magazine. The mass-production building techniques first used in Levittown became the norm in the home construction industry across the United States, and by the beginning of the new millenium, tract housing made up most of the new homes sold in the United States. The suburbs, for a great many families, had truly become the American dream.

Levittown and other suburban housing developments clearly answered a housing need, providing affordable, safe, modern homes to many middle-class consumers. However, the urban sprawl created by these suburbs grew exponentially over the years and by the early 2000s was also known for its negative aspects. According to critics, sprawl is responsible for a host of ills, among them environmental pollution, decline in the inner cities, and the destruction of rural areas and habitats. The contributors to *Current Controversies: Urban Sprawl* offer a range of opinions about the benefits and the harmful effects of urban sprawl, as well as ideas about how sprawl might be managed in the future.

CHAPTER 1

Is Urban Sprawl a Serious Problem?

Chapter Overview

Environmental Literacy Council

The Environmental Literacy Council is an independent, non-profit organization that helps students develop environmental literacy.

In the decades following World War II, rising levels of prosperity, the widespread availability of affordable transportation, and the lure of green lawns and open spaces spurred a migration of inner city populations to outer areas. Between 1970 and 1990, suburban populations grew 60 percent, while urban populations grew only 12 percent. This trend continues as families move further from the city centers in order to find lower housing costs and better quality school systems. Many businesses follow suit, motivated by easy highway access, increased parking availability, and more pronounced corporate identity. This expansion has been termed "urban sprawl," and while there are a number of definitions, it is generally considered to be low-density dispersed development outside of urban city centers.

The amount of people living in the suburbs doubled from 1900 to 1950, doubling again between 1950 and 2000. Many cities once considered to be significant urban centers within the United States, including Detroit and Philadelphia, fell victim to increased racial tensions, white flight, and the onset of suburbanization throughout the mid- to late 20th century. Although many of these 'older' cities are beginning to experience urban revitalization, they continue to lose population to their surrounding suburbs. Even in New York City, the largest city in America, we continue to see tens of thousands of people move to the suburbs each year. While the city itself had a

Environmental Literacy Council, "Urban Sprawl," May 8, 2007. www.enviroliteracy.org. Reproduced by permission.

population of over 8.2 million in 2005, the entire metropolitan area, including New York City, stood at over 18 million people.

Pros and Cons of Sprawl

There are many factors that contribute to low-density development, and it is unclear as to whether it actually contributes to or detracts from quality of life. As was seen during previous times, people continue to move from inner cities in search of safer neighborhoods, more affordable homes, better schools, and sometimes even jobs, as more and more businesses relocate to the outer fringes of many cities.

The surrounding environment is also impacted by urban sprawl.

Unfortunately, these trends can exacerbate difficulties within inner cities, which often face a declining tax base without an equal decline in the cost of city services. Therefore, many local jurisdictions have undertaken a number of initiatives to address suburbanization and urban sprawl, including zoning policies, tax incentives, and restrictions on development in outlying areas within city control. From an outlying area economic perspective, although development has a variety of benefits, sprawl can also require governments to spend millions of extra dollars to build new streets, schools, access to utilities and other services. Other critiques are considered purely aesthetic, including the proliferation of shopping centers and other commercial development along highways.

The surrounding environment is also impacted by urban sprawl. The building of roads, homes, and businesses, along with a change in the overall land use, can fragment areas and pose a threat to biodiversity in animal populations as their habitats are diminished, blocking feeding areas and altering migration patterns. This development can also lead to an increase in discharges of polluted runoff water into area streams and lakes. In areas with natural landscapes, the ground is often absorbent, trapping water and slowly filtering it into the ground, gradually moving it into waterways. In cities and suburbs, however, pavement and other covered surfaces are not able to absorb rain or runoff. Water gathers on the surface and runs off into the waterways, carrying pollutants—such as gas, oils, and fertilizers—along the way. This may also cause an increase in the speed of runoff to the point [at] which it can result in flooding and/or erosion. Finally, the shift in much of the urban population may also lead to increased air emissions due to more traveling and longer commutes in a wider regional area that may not have access to public transit.

Strategies to Control Sprawl

As the impacts of urban sprawl have become more apparent, developers have begun to look at incorporating sustainable growth and development practices. One such practice is deemed *smart growth*. The main premise of smart growth involves the design of multi-use neighborhoods that locate shops, offices, schools, parks, and other services nearer to homes, so that residents can walk, bike, or use public transportation, decreasing the dependence on cars. This method of development also provides a variety of housing options in order to promote diversity throughout the community, and uses a number of strategies to develop the land in a manner that reuses that which has already been developed, preserves much of the surrounding natural land and important environmental areas, and does its best to protect water and air quality.

Another practice taken up by several cities and states across the U.S. and Canada is to establish urban growth boundaries (UGBs) which are drawn around a city center in order to specify the limits for additional urban growth. Areas within the boundary are available for higher density urban development, while land outside of the boundary is limited to lower density development. The primary purpose of UGBs is to help preserve natural areas and resources that surround many cities, including farms, parks, and watersheds.

As urban sprawl continues to move population throughout the country, the task of planning—whether it be for urban renewal, managing city growth, or for suburbanization—will likely focus on increasing practices that incorporate smart growth and sustainable development as mainstream elements to preserving both our natural space as well as resources.

Urban Sprawl Causes a Host of Problems for U.S. Communities

Don DeGraaf, Jill Lankford, and Sam Lankford

Don DeGraaf is chairperson of the University of Oregon's Physical Department. Sam Lankford is the director of the Sustainable Tourism and Environmentalism Program (STEP) at the University of Northern Iowa. Jill Lankford is a research coordinator at STEP.

Many of the pressing problems in America's communities today [are] connected to the issues of urban sprawl, as well as what it means to be a citizen. As these issues play out, the suburbs are getting scrutinized by city officials and the general public. We are asking important questions about how to design areas to encourage a sense of community and promote the common good. These questions have been raised within the last 50 years, in which we have seen the quality of life in our inner cities deteriorate due to a wide range of inter-connected issues such as:

- Creating strip malls out of farmland in the suburbs pulls people away from central cities;

- Fewer people (especially families) in central cities leads to a smaller tax base for services including schools and parks and recreation; and

- Deteriorating schools and public places leads the middle class families to leave cities, and results in the decay of inner cities.

Don DeGraaf, Jill Lankford, and Sam Lankford, "A New Perspective on Urban Spaces: Urban Sprawl, New Urbanism and the Role of the Park and Recreation Field," *Parks & Recreation*, vol. 40, iss. 8, August 2005, pp. 56–64. www.nrpa.org. Reproduced by permission.

A Major Issue

As the 21st century unfolds, our sprawling development pattern in the U.S. has emerged as a major issue for our collective society. In dealing with sprawl author James Kuntsler has called for developing a more widespread consensus of hope—a cultural agreement as to the kind of world we want to live in, as well as the will to make this vision a reality. It is clear that the quality of the areas we build influences the quality of life in our communities.

John Muir, the great American naturalist, once stated, "When we try to pick out anything by itself, we find it hitched to everything else in the universe," and so it is with current development patterns. Development should encompass a wide range of economic, social, environmental and spiritual components, which demand an interdisciplinary and regional approach to urban design. Smart growth, new urbanism, sustainable communities, livable communities and healthy communities are current movements that address issues related to the predominant development pattern today—associated with growth, environmental degradation, inequity and an eroding quality of life. These movements all recognize the importance of regional development strategies and are seen as part of a "new regionalism."

The decay [of] . . . the public realm can be seen in . . .
the loss of the front porch in neighborhoods.

The goals of the new urbanism movement encourage governments to build social capital and address the problems of urban sprawl. New urbanism is a way to develop public space; it is about design, and recognizes that our built environment influences the way we enjoy life and how people use their community. . . .

Loss of the Public Realm

The decay or lack of attention to the public realm can be seen in a variety of ways from the loss of the front porch in neighborhoods to a lack of permanence in municipal buildings and public space. Prior to the 1940s, most houses had a front porch where people gathered and socialized with their neighbors. However as air conditioning was created, television evolved and backyards became more attractive, we have seen a movement from the front porch to the backyard and from public to private space.

Governments on all levels were also shifting their approach to building public spaces. For example, from the time of Ben Franklin to the 1940s there was an ordinance within the U.S. Postal Service that buildings needed to be built with permanence in mind (buildings were to last 250 to 300 years). Since 1945, post offices have traded down in an effort to cut costs and now have buildings that do not add to the community. Recreation departments have also experienced a similar shift in priorities.

Many central cities have experienced decline as the suburbs around them have grown rapidly.

Consider Chicago, where recreation buildings built early in the 20th century added beauty and contributed to the look of the city. Early park and recreation reformers understood that community could not form in the absence of communal space without places for people to get together to talk. Civic life requires settings in which people meet as equals. The most significant amenity that the city can offer residents is a public area where people can meet in settings that promote public discourse.

Declining Tax Base

Many central cities have experienced decline as the suburbs around them have grown rapidly. As people and wealth leave the city, its property values decline, tax rates increase, services decline, and social problems and crime often increase. This creates a downward spiral for urban areas and provides the model of throwaway communities. As central cities decline can first-ring suburbs be far behind?

In Myron Orfield's 1997 study of the Minneapolis/St. Paul area, he created a time-lapsed montage of communities bobbing up and down in successive waves of prosperity, decline and decay. These waves, moving out from the city are now lapping into the suburbs. Orfield is quick to point out that "if it can happen here, no American region is immune" and prompts the question of where will it end.

As tax bases erode in inner cities, fast-growing suburbs struggle to keep pace with development. Consider that the infrastructure (sewer, water, streets, parks, fire and police) to support this development becomes more and more expensive the farther out it stretches. For example, in a 1999 report published by the National Public Policy Education Committee in South Carolina, "if sprawl continues unchecked, statewide infrastructure costs for the period 1995 to 2015 are projected to be more than $56 billion, or $750 per citizen every year for the next 20 years."

As development sprawls, the amount of time people travel increases.

Stemming this decline is difficult and requires a wide range of partnerships that maintain the quality of life in cities and neighborhoods. Recreation and leisure opportunities are an important component in promoting the good life. As Michael Leitner and Sara Leitner report in their 1996 book, *Leisure En-*

hancement: "leisure behavior is the most important or one of the most important determinants of life satisfaction and psychological well being."

Automobile Dependency

As development sprawls, the amount of time people travel increases. In the U.S., where mass transit is underdeveloped, a large portion of the day is spent in transit. According to Michael deCourcy Hinds' *A Nice Place to Live: Creating Communities, Fighting Sprawl,* the amount of time Americans spend driving automobiles has increased 60 percent since 1980. In addition, new developments are planned with cars in mind, meaning bigger parking lots, larger roads, air pollution and the erosion of walkways. Harvard Public Policy Professor Robert Putnam notes that each additional 10 minutes spent in daily commuting time cuts community involvement by 10 percent.

A 2003 report from the Surface Transportation Policy Project shows that America's families spend more than 19 cents out of every dollar earned on transportation—an expense second only to housing and greater than food and healthcare combined. The nation's poorest families are particularly burdened, spending more than 40 percent of their take-home pay just to get around.

Health-Related Risks

Sedentary living habits have increased in the last 20 years with the increase in desk jobs and the lack of exercise in peoples' day-to-day lives. The increasing use of automobiles has decreased physical activity, contributing to poor health and the rising level of obesity in the U.S. It is estimated that physical inactivity and obesity are contributing factors in 300,000 to 500,000 deaths each year in the U.S.

There has been an increase in the prevalence of obesity among adults in the U.S. throughout the last 20 years, adding more than $100 billion a year to our national healthcare costs. Nationwide, the proportion of children ages 6 to 18 that were overweight increased from 6 percent in 1976–1980 to 15 percent in 1999–2000. Alarmingly, one in every seven kids is overweight in the U.S.

Design of cities and neighborhoods can encourage people to walk often and for relatively longer periods. For example, residents of urban areas living in houses that were built prior to 1974 are more likely to get exercise by walking than peers living in newer homes. A recent study published in the *American Journal of Preventive Medicine* found that the link between walking and house age was present in urban and suburban areas but not in rural areas.

The study also found that what makes older neighborhoods special is that homes are built close together making walking easy and time efficient. Older neighborhoods mix homes with businesses and parks, which encourages walking over driving. Sidewalks and the safety of streets also encourage more walking. Newer neighborhoods usually have wider streets than do older ones, which leads to higher speeds for auto traffic.

According to public health professionals, one of the most effective interventions is regular, physical activity such as bicycling and walking as well as leading an active life. . . .

Environmental Problems

As sprawl increases our reliance on the automobile and often works to undermine general health, it also contributes to poor water and air quality. A sprawling development pattern often undermines the benefits provided by a healthy ecosystem such as water and air purification, mitigation of floods and droughts, detoxification and decomposition of waste, soil generation and fertility and climate stabilization.

Urban development typically negates these services with the loss of wetlands and the creation of impervious surfaces.

Watershed planning that is coordinated with recreation planning can reduce non-point source pollution, contribute to aquifer recharge, mitigate floods and droughts and provide for habitat diversity.

The park system within a community should be considered a part of the overall infrastructure and an investment in the community's natural capital. A wall-planned park system is coordinated with municipal water management, transportation planning and energy conservation. Park and recreation departments have long been stewards of our natural heritage in cities. Typically, they are the largest land managers within a community. Accomplishing this role requires active participation in land use and site development decisions.

Loss of Social Capital

The idea of "social capital" has received a great deal of attention since the release of Putnam's book *Bowling Alone: The Collapse and Revival of American Community*. In this book, Putnam reviews the "state of community" and concludes that America is suffering from a decline in social capital.

Putnam defines social capital as "features of social life—networks, norms and trust—that enable participants to act together more effectively to purpose shared objectives." This is a critical element to the success of democracy. Putnam documents the decline of social capital in America as reflected by decreasing membership in voluntary organizations, such as the Boy Scouts of America, the League of Women Voters, the Parent Teacher Association and the American Red Cross.

Putnam attributes our loss of social capital to a variety of factors such as changing work patterns, urban sprawl, generational change, television and other changes in technology. Regardless of the cause, social capital is an important issue for leisure service professionals and can be identified as one of the benefits of our programs and services. Consider, in a 1996 study of conflict and violence in and around public housing in Chicago, researchers found that the residents of buildings with surrounding green space had a stronger sense of community, had better relationships with their neighbors, and reported using less violent ways of dealing with domestic conflicts, particularly with their parents.

As we move forward into the 21st century, Putnam suggests the need to get creative in addressing the decline of social capital.

Urban Sprawl Destroys Habitat and Farmland and Harms Biodiversity

Cynthia Berlin

Cynthia Berlin is an assistant professor in the Department of Geography and Earth Science, University of Wisconsin-La Crosse. She specializes in the application of satellite remote sensing and GIS to environmental geography.

Urban sprawl, or simply sprawl, is no longer the relatively exclusive domain of city planners and developers; it has worked its way into the everyday life of the average American. Popularized by the news media, urban sprawl is now a regular topic of conversation and debate in homes throughout the country. Almost everyone has an opinion on sprawl and many people are quick to volunteer ideas on how to solve "the problem." But there is no popular consensus on what urban sprawl means and little public awareness of its myriad of impacts. Definitions are often vague and poorly conceptualized. They range from the meaningless "I know it when I see it" to somewhat more studied statements of "vehicle-dependent development" or "uncontrolled urban expansion." Definitions like these often enhance a misunderstanding of the full meaning and complexity of urban sprawl. Although most people agree that sprawl destroys natural habitat, consumes prime agricultural land and limits outdoor recreational opportunities, few are aware of the full scope of sprawl's impacts.

Sprawl in Small Communities

It is often assumed that urban sprawl is just a careless spreading out of development from a large urban center. This overly simple definition is frequently perpetuated by the news media,

Cynthia Berlin, "Sprawl Comes to the American Heartland," *Focus*, vol. 46, iss. 4, spring 2002, pp. 2–10. Copyright © 2002 American Geographical Society. Reproduced by permission.

and to some degree, by planners and developers as well. Such a poorly conceived definition leads to a misunderstanding of the intricacies of sprawl and sets the stage for conflicts between developers and antisprawl (or pro-smart growth) advocates. Furthermore, two things are assumed by accepting this incomplete definition: first, that sprawl lacks any unique geographic characteristics, and second, that it is a problem confronting only major metropolitan areas such as Los Angeles, New York, or Atlanta. Both of these assumptions are false. Although sprawl may be haphazard in its nature, it does have some fundamental spatial characteristics and patterns that cannot be ignored. Also, sprawl is not restricted to major metropolitan areas. Sprawl is a serious problem for smaller cities (with populations of approximately 50,000 or less) and their nearby exurban and rural communities. However, comparatively little attention has been focused on these areas. This is likely due to a multitude of reasons but near the top of the list are most probably three factors: (1) the news media tends to favor stories that confirm the evils of big cities (small-town life is in many respects romanticized), (2) sprawl is a relatively recent phenomenon to these smaller communities, and (3) there is a large amount of readily accessible data on major metropolitan areas.

The growth fringe that surrounds the greater La Crosse, Wisconsin metropolitan area in many respects typifies the type of area often overlooked in the sprawl debate. This region includes approximately 1,600 square miles in western Wisconsin and southeastern Minnesota and has a population of about 170,000. Development around the smaller towns and in the rural areas is rapidly expanding as more people move into new growth areas that are scattered throughout the landscape. Most residents of the region agree that urban sprawl is consuming more and more agricultural land and natural habitat. However, there has been little consistent effort to either quantify the loss of open space or examine the geographic characteristics of the development patterns for the region. Without these assessments, the assumption that sprawl is occurring is qualitative speculation.

What Is Sprawl?

Sprawl can be defined with quantitative measures as well as with more qualitative descriptors. Although both types of definitions are useful and provide valuable insight into sprawl, they are not without shortcomings.

Throughout the U.S., prime farmland is being lost to development at an alarming rate.

The most popular definitions of sprawl rely on quantifying urbanization in some way that relates it to decreases in population density or increased vehicle use.

The Sierra Club, in *Sprawl: The Dark Side of the American Dream* (1997), defines sprawl as automobile-dependent low-density development extending out from the urban fringe. Sprawl is often expressed in the form of a sprawl index. One of the most common indices uses the generally accepted assumption that sprawl occurs when the rate of land consumption for development exceeds the population growth rate for an area. This has been the basis for numerous studies made by the Sierra Club. Various combinations of population density and vehicle miles traveled to quantify sprawl have served as a basis for many studies of sprawl in large metropolitan areas throughout the United States. *USA Today* developed its own sprawl index based on population density (February 22, 2001). Using U.S. Census Bureau data, *USA Today* ranked the nation's 271 metropolitan areas on a scale from 2 (no sprawl) to 542 (maximum sprawl).

As useful as these definitions are to quantifying the amount of land lost to development and assessing changes in population density, they do not fully explore what sprawl involves. In some cases, relying solely on quantitative indices of sprawl can produce potentially misleading results. For example, by including the planned functional (public) open space of metropolitan areas in the calculations of its sprawl index, the *USA Today* study came to the controversial conclusion that Portland, Oregon has more sprawl than Los Angeles. But functional open space is generally considered a positive result of "smart" planning, not a characteristic of sprawl. Most experts on urban sprawl propose several descriptive factors that provide a more complete definition of sprawl than only considering low population densities. These include:

- leapfrog or scattered development

- commercial strip development

- single-use development

- poor accessibility and automobile dependency (e.g. lack of public transport)

- fragmented open space between scattered developments

- lack of functional open space (public space that provides high-quality habitat)

- high edge contrast (e.g. a strip mall next to a wetland)

- lack of nearby conveniences (e.g. businesses, shopping, and services)

- increasing expenditures on infrastructure (e.g. roads, utilities, services).

Providing infrastructure and services to scattered developments may actually force communities to spend more than increases in tax revenue can generate.

As with the sprawl indices, descriptive definitions of sprawl are not without limitations. The primary problem with descriptive definitions is that they are basically qualitative statements. Terms such as scattered, trip, poor, low and high are relative and a review of the sprawl literature suggests that there is some disagreement on what these adjectives actually mean. It is difficult to quantify these factors in a way that eliminates this problem. Indices that measure some of these factors can be, and have been, developed, but interpretations of the numerical results are subjective. Nonetheless, qualitative descriptors of sprawl provide important insights into its spatial pattern and should not be discounted.

The Costs of Sprawl

The most obvious cost of sprawl is the destruction of natural habitat and farmland. The loss of natural habitat is acknowledged as a serious threat to biodiversity and an immediate concern for conservation. Wetlands are drained, forests cut down, and grasslands paved over in the name of progress. The consequences extend well beyond decreases in biodiversity. Wetland losses now contribute to increases in the frequency and severity of flood events. Many residents of the La Crosse, Wisconsin region are concerned that the loss of wetlands and other non-developed land, including farmland, increases the region's risk to flooding. The removal of trees and other natural vegetation aggravates soil erosion and increases stream sedimentation. Increases in sediment deposits in the Mississippi River in this region contribute to the rising cost of dredging to maintain a navigable channel. Throughout the U.S., prime farmland is being lost to development at an alarming rate and what survives is increasingly fragmented. According to the American Farmland Trust, 70 percent of our best farmland lies directly in the path of development. As existing roads are expanded and more highways are built, development into rural areas is facilitated.

It is often assumed that development of any type (including sprawl) brings communities financial benefits by strengthening the local tax base. While this may have been true during the 1970s and 1980s, today [2002] the increased costs of providing infrastructure and services to scattered developments may actually force communities to spend more than increases in tax revenue can generate. These costs are not only associated with building and maintaining more roads, and extending utilities, but also in providing such basic services as fire and police protection to developments that are often widely dispersed. Because many of the single-use developments are residential areas that have drawn families out of more densely populated town centers, existing city schools are often closed while new schools are built in the outer suburbs. The cost of these and other service-related construction projects can quickly eat away tax revenues.

Urban Sprawl Is Partially to Blame for the Nation's Obesity Problem

Brian Johnson

Brian Johnson is a writer for Finance and Commerce Daily Newspaper, *a daily newspaper in Minneapolis, Minnesota, devoted exclusively to business matters.*

It's a common lament that urban sprawl is bad for the environment. But what does it do to your waistline? Dr. Reid Ewing, a research professor with the National Center for Smart Growth at the University of Maryland, told a gathering at the University of Minnesota this week that low-density development associated with sprawl is partially to blame for rising levels of obesity. "What's causing us to be heavier when we live in a sprawling environment? Our explanation is that it's our daily lives," Ewing said. "What we do when we go buy a loaf of bread, or go out for lunch—that's making the difference. We're active in a walkable environment, we're inactive as part of our daily routines in a sprawling environment."

A Study of Sprawl and Obesity

Ewing reached those conclusions after working on a study that linked sprawl with weight gain. The study, first published in September 2003, gained widespread media attention and put Ewing in the national spotlight. The report, "Measuring the Health Effects of Sprawl—A National Analysis of Physical Activity, Obesity, and Chronic Disease," concluded that people in areas associated with sprawl—low-density development, poor pedestrian infrastructure, etc.—tend to be heavier because they lead a more sedentary, automobile-dependent lifestyle.

"It's not all a matter of diet," Ewing said. "We know that the energy equation has two sides—it's not just what you eat, it's how active you are. We have absolutely, in my view, incontrovertible evidence that the built environment affects our travel choices."

The report estimated that 65 percent of adults in the United States are overweight and that nearly one in three are obese. Using data from the U.S. Census Bureau and other sources, the report's researchers developed a numerical index to measure the degree of sprawl in 448 U.S. counties. Scores ranged from 63 to 352, with the higher numbers indicating the least sprawl. The study, using a national health survey, compared the health of 200,000 people living in those counties with the level of sprawl in their respective counties. Age, income and other factors were taken into account.

The Verdict?

People in counties with the highest degree of sprawl tend to be 6 pounds heavier than their counterparts in higher-density areas. Among other conclusions, the report also found that a person is 6 percent more likely to have hypertension for every 50-point increase in the level of sprawl in their area.

Critics say the research is biased toward the smart growth agenda . . . and the relationship between obesity and suburban sprawl development is tenuous at best.

Looking at Minnesota, Isanti County had the highest level of sprawl and Ramsey was the least "sprawling" county. According to the report, the expected probability of obesity is 19.1 percent in Isanti County, 17.4 percent in Ramsey. The report also concludes that Isanti County residents are slightly more likely (24.6 percent probability versus 23.4 percent) than people in Ramsey County to suffer from hypertension.

The Critics' Views

Not everyone is swayed by the report. Critics say the research is biased toward the smart growth agenda, that the differences—even if you accept the data—are minor, and that the relationship between obesity and suburban sprawl development is tenuous at best.

Randal O'Toole, a senior economist with the Thoreau Institute and an outspoken critic of the "smart growth" philosophy, said the effort to link sprawl with obesity is fraught with problems. "If you look at the larger research, you find that there's a lot of things that affect obesity," he said. "Lower income people tend to be more obese than higher income. Education is important. Suburbs versus cities have a trivial impact."

Higher densities, shortened streets, mixed land uses, strong city centers, and improved pedestrian infrastructure . . . make cities more walkable.

Although the Ewing study controlled for factors like education and income, O'Toole said, "You can't adjust for everything. So you're going to get noise in the data. All you're going to prove, maybe, is that suburbs have people who are older, or are in some other category that leads to obesity. To me, it's all junk science. They (smart growth advocates) are using it to promote a political agenda. They don't want people to have the freedom to choose to live in a house with a nice backyard."

A Challenge for City Planners

Ewing conceded that the study doesn't prove that sprawl makes people heavy or sick. "It's a correlation, a statistical association between the two," he said. "We've got a long way to go before we've sort of proven this connection. Does it actually cause (weight gain), or are there other factors? Is there a threshold?

Do you have to be above a certain density before you get any benefit? Does sprawl affect diet? These are all important issues that are being researched right now."

At least four studies that examine the relationship between sprawl and weight gain have already been published, Ewing said, and he predicted that there will be 30 or 40 studies out within five years. "We already know (from other studies) that kids living on cul-de-sacs are more active," he said. "That flies in the face of this notion that we want highly interconnected streets to make adults more physically active. But maybe it's different for kids. You're going to be absolutely inundated with this kind of information. For urban planners, this is going to be the big issue for the next decade, I think. It's going to be like the environment was in the '70s and new urbanism was in the 1990s. It's going to be just huge."

Higher densities, shortened streets, mixed land uses, strong city centers, and improved pedestrian infrastructure are among the planning strategies that make cities more walkable and less "sprawling," according to Ewing. He cited Portland, Ore., as a model for that type of planning. "Portland has, in their rules and laws, made it advantageous for communities to increase densities," he said. "When they started growth management in Oregon, the average lot size was 13,000 square feet. It is now 7,000. There's a lot of dense development in the Portland area. It's done through changes in zoning, which were imposed on localities by the metropolitan government and the state."

Urban Sprawl Also Afflicts Developing Countries

Neha Menon

Neha Menon is a student at the School of Forestry and Environmental Studies, Yale University, in Cambridge, Massachusetts.

Urban sprawl has been recognized as a problem that faces the developed world. There has been a growing concern about this issue among planners, policy makers, environmentalists, citizen groups, etc. As the developing world urbanizes, more often than not, the model of development chosen is the Western one. Most developing countries follow their erstwhile colonial masters into development. While this model does have its positive aspects, it also has a large number of fallouts, one of the most important being an increasingly consumption oriented economy. Developing countries are fast moving along the same unsustainable consumption path. As they develop, the ratio of urban to rural land is increasing. By 2030, it is projected that almost 60% of the world's population will be urban. In such a context, it is important to realize that developing countries are also inheriting a large number of developed country problems.

The problem of urban sprawl is not restricted to the developed world. It exists in the developing world also. However, the indicators are different as are the causes for sprawl. Developing country sprawl is largely a result of necessity: people move to the city in search of better employment and opportunity. This leads to a burgeoning city sprawl well beyond the limits of the city. One of the main differences between urban sprawl in developed and developing countries is that in developed countries, people do not want to live in the cities: they

Neha Menon, "Urban Sprawl: A Developing Country Approach," *Vision*, May 7, 2004. www.wscsd.org/ejournal. Reproduced by permission of the author.

choose to move out. However, in developing countries, people move out because there is not enough space for them to live in the city. . . .

The Move from Rural to Urban Areas

The onset of the new millennium has seen, for the first time, more people living in urban areas than rural. This is a rising trend seen the world over, especially in developing countries. Though once seen as islands, cities can no longer be thought to stand apart. As it becomes clear that the world is unquestionably a globalized one, it is also becoming clear that it is increasingly an urbanized one. Three billion people live in cities today, and it is projected that by 2030, nearly 60% of the world's population will be urban. Also, estimates say that by 2030, most of the cities in the list of the top thirty will be from developing countries. The current worldwide rate for urbanization is 0.8%, ranging from 0.3% for developed countries to 1.6% for Africa.

Sprawl in developed countries is usually a matter of preference.

The issues associated with urbanization in developing countries pose a challenge, merely because the dynamic and the context in which they occur are very different from those in which the now-developed countries urbanized. Therefore, the solutions proposed must take into account the differences—and adapt to the specific situation that they are being applied in. Unfortunately, this is rarely the case. As a result, developing countries end up further complicating the issue, instead of resolving it. Often, the solution is a short-term one, and the problem persists. This has led to unsustainable patterns of growth in the Third World. The basic problem with developing country growth strategies is that they are usually modeled on the Western model of development. There is a growing realization that this pattern of growth is highly unsustainable and that there is a need for alternative, more sustainable methods of growth. If the entire world were to consume resources at the same rate as the USA, we would need three planets to satisfy the demand.

Cities in the developing world are growing in both size and number. However, they cannot expand indefinitely. Every kind of growth has a limiting resource; in this case, the limiting factor is land. As the rate of urbanization increases, the patterns of land use are changing. Cities are using land that was formerly used as agricultural land or was habitat for biodiversity. These changes in land use patterns are characteristic of the phenomenon of urban sprawl. According to the Vermont Forum on Sprawl, "Sprawl is dispersed, auto-dependent development outside of compact urban and village centers, along highways, and in rural countryside."

This interpretation of the term is based on observations made in developed countries and is indicative of the fact that sprawl is usually seen as a problem that affects developed countries, primarily the USA. This is not the case. Urban sprawl is increasingly becoming an issue in developing countries as well. This has led to a change in land use patterns and the spatial cover of cities. It promotes inefficient use of land, energy as well as encroachment on agricultural land. This change in land use patterns is easiest to observe on the periphery of the cities. As cities continue to experience unplanned growth, the built area at the city limits is increasing. This is fragmenting land, adversely affecting agricultural land, green space, groundwater, etc. This is also causing a negative impact on conservation of habitat. There are a number of definitions that have been put forth to explain the concept of sprawl. However, most of them cater to the developed country notion of sprawl, like the one stated above. Cities in developing countries face a problem of unregulated and unplanned growth beyond city limits. Urban sprawl in the developing world can be seen as a spread of new development on vacant land (which has not been used for urban purposes), as a result of increased population within the city. It is not a problem of large sprawling cities—quite the contrary. The cities are more compact than in the developed world. However, the demand for space and inefficient use of land within cities leads to sprawling growth.

In a developing country, sprawl is fueled more by necessity.

However, since the indicators of sprawl are different from those in the developed world, it is often assumed that sprawl is a problem only in developed countries.

Causes of Sprawl

Some of the more generic causes of sprawl are population growth, increasing incomes, subsidization of infrastructure investments like roads, etc., and physical constraints on development. There is one basic difference between the causes of sprawl in a developed country and that in a developing country: sprawl in developed countries is usually a matter of preference. It may have begun with the industrial revolution, and was later reinforced by government policies. An important factor contributing to sprawl is the fact that the incomes of the people in developed countries are extremely high, as compared to those in developing countries. This facilitates the move from urban to suburban areas. People have come to prefer moving to open spaces at reasonable distances from cities. It has now become an inherent pattern of life for a large majority of people, and is therefore difficult to change. Another problem this has led to is the growth pf dependence on automobiles. The entire culture in developed countries (especially the USA) is centered around automobile use. This coupled with government policies that encourage the move to suburban areas, and subsidize the use of private transport has fueled urban sprawl in the developed world to a great extent. Solutions and approaches to deal with sprawl in developed countries must deal with changing attitudes and lifestyles of people. This is easier said than done.

If not checked, [sprawl in developing countries] will lead to consequences that are far worse than those seen in the developed world.

The story in developing countries is . . . different. In a developing country, sprawl is fueled more by necessity. A lot of the underlying causal factors are historical, and have built up over a number of years. Sprawl, in this case, is concentrated around certain pockets of dense human population—the major metros. The causes of sprawl here too can be traced to historical reasons—most often to the colonial legacy that most developing countries have. Major metros were developed as administrative centers, transportation hubs, where people from the hinterland came in search of employment and stayed on. These became central cities after the colonial masters left. The growth of these major metros was unplanned and gradual. This trend has continued into the post-colonial period too. Most of these metro cities remain the dominant source of employment, education, etc., and therefore people still migrate here from the rural areas. Since the majority of the population is poor and in need of employment, they usually move to the metros to look for a better standard of life. This has led to burgeoning centers of urbanization that are growing outward, away from the city centre. However, as these countries urbanize at rapid rates, these pockets are increasing and so is the problem of sprawl. Another key issue here is the problem of population growth. Most of the developing countries are at that stage in their demographic transition when their fertility rate is rising and the mortality rate is declining. Thus the population is growing and will continue to grow for at least the next fifty years. This will have a significant impact on rural-urban migration, and therefore contribute to sprawl.

An interesting observation about sprawl in developed and developing countries can be made from the ecological footprint analyses of countries. This is the application of the 80-20 rule. The proportion of people moving away from cities in the developed world constitute a small per cent of the world population in numbers, but are majority consumers of world resources. However, in developing countries, those proportions are reversed—there are a greater number of people causing sprawl in terms of sheer proportion of world population. At the same time, they use a small proportion of world resources . . .

It is clear that sprawl is increasingly becoming an issue that is associated with urbanization—whether it takes place in the developed world or the developing. However, since the context in which it takes place is very different, so are the patterns of urban sprawl. Developing countries do not have the same causes and indicators of sprawl, as do developed countries. This has led to the belief that sprawl is a problem of the developed world, which is far from true. It does exist, and if not checked, will lead to consequences that are far worse than those seen in the developed world today.

Urban Sprawl Is the American Dream

Rachel Dicarlo

Rachel Dicarlo is a fellow at the Phillips Foundation, a nonprofit organization founded to advance constitutional principles, a democratic society, and a vibrant free enterprise system.

Consider the much-maligned American suburb. For decades now, it has been mocked by authors and intellectuals as the sterile, soul-crushing birthplace of such cultural blights as McMansions and strip malls. Hollywood, too, has caught on. Witness the success of the Oscar-winning movie "American Beauty" and the Emmy-winning TV show "Desperate Housewives." Both depict everyone in suburbia as somehow weird or depraved. In recent years a whole movement has coalesced, the so-called New Urbanism, to sneer at suburban sprawl and all its various progeny.

Yet as Robert Bruegmann shows in *Sprawl: A Compact History*, the conventional anti-suburbs wisdom is often just plain wrong. Mr. Bruegmann, a professor of urban planning and art history at the University of Illinois, takes every assumption about "sprawl"—a pejorative to be sure—and turns it on its head. Many of the characteristics associated with sprawl—such as low-density development and lack of regional or public-use planning—he argues, have been present in prosperous cities since the beginning of urban history. They are the natural effects of a city's gaining economic maturity—not the recent consequence of vulgar Americans insisting on living in monstrous, single-use homes, as many sprawl detractors purport. As Mr. Bruegmann persuasively demonstrates, people and businesses have always had good reasons for wanting to leave the city.

Rachel Dicarlo, "Sprawl: A Compact History," *The Washington Times*, December 11, 2005. www.robertbruegmann.com/_images/reviews/WashingtonTimes.pdf. Reproduced by permission.

Sprawl in Early History

Take Ancient Rome. Like most cities, Rome can credit its existence to felicitous geography: a piece of land that could be easily defended; a safe harbor; and rapids that could be harnessed and used for power. Mobility was a problem for all but the richest Romans, so most urban functions—residential, industrial and commercial—lay in close proximity to one another. Walls that reinforced and protected the city compounded the density problem. Beyond the city walls was what the Romans called suburbium, a vast parcel of land that accommodated industries the city could not, such as pottery works, burial grounds and slaughterhouses. Here lived the poorest residents of Rome, people who couldn't afford municipal services or the security of the walls. At the other end of the spectrum, many wealthy Romans kept villas in suburbium, which offered a getaway reprieve from the grimy, crowded city. "Ancient, medieval, and early modern literature is filled with stories of the elegant life of a privileged aristocracy living for large parts of the year in villas and hunting lodges at the periphery of large cities," Mr. Bruegmann writes.

In the United States, the real push outward came . . . when blue-collar families discovered the allure of cheap land and lower taxes beyond the city limits.

Similar patterns appeared throughout the West and China as early as the Ming Dynasty. London, for example, the biggest economy in the Western world, maintained its population in the 17th and 18th centuries despite mass suburban and exurban development beyond its walls primarily because peasants continued to arrive from the countryside. English "sprawl"—in the form of large country estates—formed the literary backdrop for such romantic writers as Jane Austen and the Brontë sisters.

Sprawl in the United States

In the United States, the real push outward came during the interwar boom years, when blue-collar families discovered the allure of cheap land and lower taxes beyond the city limits. The rise of car ownership and the construction of superhighways gave many the option of moving out of the city to live in a detached house with a yard. If they did most of the building work themselves, they could become homeowners. These opportunities helped create a booming middle class.

But after World War II, factories and industrial jobs, especially in the northeastern "Rust Belt," headed for the suburbs or disappeared altogether. Indeed, it was many of the policies that sprawl critics now embrace—high taxes, union wages, regulation—that drove them outward. As jobs and citizens left town, large numbers of buildings were abandoned. Some of the buildings were bulldozed, the space used for parking garages or parking lots; others, in the wake of nostalgia for city life, were renovated and turned into expensive, "historic district" condos. In places like Baltimore's Canton, Philadelphia's Central City or Manhattan's Greenwich Village, living in a converted factory—with high ceilings, oddly shaped windows and exposed brick walls—is now a hallmark of sophistication. So-called historic districts have proliferated. Sidewalk benches, cobblestone streets and traditional streetlights have been either maintained or restored. Meanwhile, as the factories disappeared, so, increasingly, did such urban irritants as pollution, bleak industrial landscapes and truck traffic. "What few people seemed to notice," Mr. Bruegmann writes, "was the way the rising fortunes of the center . . . were directly connected to developments at the edge." That is, as more affordable housing became available in the suburbs—allowing the middle classes to live there—the wealthy were more inclined to stay in the cities, particularly since many prestigious jobs in law, medicine and business remained there. For the most part, the richest Americans continue to populate the densest parts of an urban area, like Park Avenue in Manhattan or Beacon Hill in Boston. They can afford to make the trade- off—higher taxes and bad public schools for urban cultural and social stimulation.

Debunking Sprawl Myths

Mr. Bruegmann also addresses the myths that sprawl detractors and "smart growth" advocates have fostered to claim suburban life is ruining cities. Are the suburbs expanding at an ever-increasing rate? Not really. It's true some farms and forests have been converted into subdivisions, but right now [2005] suburban and exurban development is flat. Outward development is inevitable as the number of households increases and city governments make policies hostile to taxpayers. And the big picture is that 90 percent of America remains open space. Census Bureau statistics obscure that fact. Once part of a county near a city becomes populous enough the Census Bureau will make the entire county part of a metropolitan area even if large parts of it are rural.

But if we limited growth, wouldn't we relieve traffic congestion and pollution? It's a mystery how this argument ever got any traction. Trapping more people into a tighter space can only make pollution and traffic congestion worse. Indeed, traffic tends to be the thickest in metropolitan areas like New York, Washington, D.C., and Los Angeles, where politicians have refused to build new roads to accommodate more drivers.

Do the suburbs trap women? The suburbs give women, like everyone else, a choice. Central planners and cultural elites don't like to hear arguments about choice because they think that given a choice, ordinary citizens will usually make the wrong one. Moreover, the rise of car ownership, particularly in car-friendly suburban areas, has made life easier for a lot of women. Imagine toting two kids around on a rainy

Tuesday, from school to soccer practice, then to the grocery store, then to the dry-cleaner, by riding around on light rail.

What about the hideous industrial parks that ruin the landscape? They provide great benefits for workers. Industrial parks have in fact narrowed the workplace-environment gap between white-collar and blue-collar jobs. They may still be home to vocations that are monotonous, dispiriting and dangerous, but at least the workers there have large, clean facilities that would have been the envy of workers 100 years ago, most of whom toiled away in filthy, cramped factories.

The suburbs aren't a deviation from the American Dream—they are the American Dream.

And those chain-store-heavy shopping centers with their mega-parking lots? They're not even anti-urban. Some of the first suburban shopping centers were developed by the same investors who built the downtown department stores. And, as Mr. Bruegmann points out, suburban centers took the idea of the old urban galleria and made it better. The giant parking lots make the stores more accessible to mothers with children in tow and other pedestrians. Some downtown businesses have responded to these strip malls by remodeling their shopping streets to make them more pedestrian-friendly. If that's not convincing enough, think about what smart growth would do to all those chain stores: Eliminate them in favor of higher priced urban retail outlets.

Then there are those who say that more Americans would be able to enjoy city life if only the government would stop building highways, pour money into mass transit and triple the gasoline tax to discourage driving. But that experiment has already been tried in Europe with little success, as anyone who has ever been on the highways in London or Paris during rush hour can attest. In the course of demolishing such anti-sprawl shibboleths, Mr. Bruegmann repeatedly emphasizes the cardinal virtue of American suburbia. To wit, the suburbs have made it possible for ordinary Americans to enjoy the privacy, space, leisure time and choice that were once available only to the richest of the rich. The suburbs aren't a deviation from the American Dream—they are the American Dream.

Many Suburbs Are Neighborhoods that Provide Good Places to Live

Terry O'Neill

Terry O'Neill was the editor of The Report, *a magazine that was published by Citizens Centre for Freedom and Democracy, a Canadian nonprofit organization that promotes responsible government.*

I write to you . . . from the heart of what some of my fellow citizens describe as "urban sprawl." I, on the other hand, prefer to use words of a more gentle and graceful sort. "Neighbourhood" is one such word. "Community" is another.

Now the fast-growing section of Coquitlam, B.C. [Canada] in which we live may not be the sort of archetypal mom-at-home, and kids-on-bikes neighbourhood that kids of my generation grew up in half a century ago. And neither is it the type of community represented by optimistic 1960s television situation-comedy shows. No "Beavers" here, but there do seem to be all-too-many replicants of "Beavis and Butthead."

Nevertheless, Eagle Ridge is most definitely a neighbourhood, and it is certainly part of a community. And it is mine. That is why I took such umbrage when the *Vancouver Sun* recently used the term "urban sprawl" in a caption below a photograph showing the neighbourhood in which we have lived for more than two decades now. Look closely at the picture, which illustrates a feature page examining civic election issues, and you can see the O'Neill family home, there on the left-hand side, about two-thirds of the way up. Obviously, some deep thinker in the *Sun's* downtown newsroom figured that a large concentration of relatively new single-family homes constitutes "urban sprawl." The implication is that—because urban sprawl is, by definition, ugly, undesirable and detestable—the neighbourhood represents some sort of ghastly mistake and, therefore, should not exist.

A Good Place to Live

When I look at the picture, however, I do not see a travesty of urban planning, but well-maintained homes shaded by trees first planted as seedlings by hopeful newlyweds 20 years ago. The homes are built along gently curving roads, on the side of a pleasingly pitched slope, with parks, walking paths, two schools and an abundance of green space. Hardly a planner's worst nightmare.

There is also one very practical reason why suburbs . . . are so popular: the land is relatively inexpensive.

Yes, the area is too reliant on cars, but on the whole it is a good place to live. Indeed, it represents the fulfilled dreams of many average Canadians—two-car garages, enough space in the backyard for the children to frolic, just enough privacy to allow them to keep to themselves if that is what they want, but sufficient density to foster friendships and associations at many levels. From soccer moms and foster fathers, to schoolkids and rink rats, it is home to typical Canadians living typical lives in typical surroundings.

There is also one very practical reason why suburbs such as ours are so popular: the land is relatively inexpensive. Everyone would love to live in a waterfront mansion or hobby-farm estate, but not many of us can afford to. A typical suburban home is the best we can do, and we are not complaining.

Alternatives to Urban Sprawl Unnacceptable

Am I feeling defensive about all this? You bet. Why? Because I believe that the use of such terms as "urban sprawl," to describe perfectly good neighbourhoods such as ours, represents an elitist, central-planning mentality that is, at its technocratic heart, a destructive force. Ask yourself this: If our well-planned, well-laid-out neighbourhood of single-family homes represents a grotesque affront to everything that is good and decent, then what are the alternatives? The answers are chilling.

One is a world of high-rise apartment blocks, which stack family upon family in efficient but confining quarters. In such a "perfect" urban world, we all would no doubt live in a few square miles of a densely populated city, leaving as small a "footprint" as possible on Mother Nature. The birds, bees, deer and bear would get to frolic in a boundless natural playground, while we, on the other hand, would be de facto prisoners in a de facto human zoo. In the extreme we would walk everywhere or use public transit; our kids—if we cared to have any—would be raised in efficient and compact daycares; and we would all work for the government in one form or another.

The depopulation scenario . . . is profoundly anti-human.

The other putative alternative to the "urban sprawl" bogeyman is that the world be depopulated. If there were fewer people, the argument goes, then we could all live in a more "natural" state, growing our own crops in communion with our surroundings, and all that sort of stuff.

But both these alternatives are unacceptable. The depopulation scenario, although advanced by hardcore environmental enthusiasts, is profoundly anti-human, and carries with it the implied threat of euthanasia or genocide. It is simply a no-go. The "stack 'em higher" plan is by far the most popular among trendy urban planners and left-leaning theorists, but it is a soul-destroying scheme that would transform us into automatons whose only purpose is to serve the State. You want to live in a beehive, then this is for you.

So, rather than decry urban sprawl, we just might want to celebrate it. Sure, new suburban development is all-too-often accompanied by growing pains, but those can be remedied. And anyway, what is really important is that new hopes are about new families, new dreams, and the hope that the sacrifices of today—in paying down mortgages and raising up children—will lead to a brighter future. In that light, every new home that is built, every new street that is carved out of forest, every new neighbourhood that asserts itself on the countryside, is a celebration of our humanity. And that is good. Let the sprawl go on!

Concerns About Urban Sprawl Are Class-Based Objections to Middle-Class Developments

Robert Bruegmann

Robert Bruegmann is an architectural historian, a professor and chairman of art history at the University of Illinois at Chicago, and author of the book Sprawl: A Compact History, *from which this essay is adapted.*

There is overwhelming evidence that urban sprawl has been beneficial for many people. Year after year, the vast majority of Americans respond to batteries of polls by saying that they are quite happy with where they live, whether it is a city, suburb, or elsewhere. Most objective indicators about American urban life are positive. We are more affluent than ever; home ownership is up; life spans are up; pollution is down; crime in most cities has declined. Even where sprawl has created negative consequences, it has not precipitated any crisis.

So what explains the power of today's anti-sprawl crusade? How is it possible that a prominent lawyer could open a recent book with the unqualified assertion that "sprawl is America's most lethal disease"? Worse than drug use, crime, unemployment, and poverty? Why has a campaign against sprawl expanded into a major political force across America and much of the economically advanced world?

The Problem of High Expectations

I would argue that worries about sprawl have become so vivid not because conditions are really as bad as the critics suggest, but precisely because conditions are so good. During boom years, expectations can easily run far ahead of any possibility of fulfilling them. A fast-rising economy often produces a revolution of expectations. I believe these soaring expectations are responsible for many contemporary panics.

Sprawl is where other people live, particularly people with less good taste.

Consider, for a moment, the thunderous din of complaints about traffic in Los Angeles. From one perspective, this reaction is bizarre. Even when speeds on the freeway decline to 20 miles per hour, drivers throughout the Los Angeles area move much more quickly than they do by car or public transportation at the center of almost any large, older industrial city in Europe or the U.S. It is clearly not that congestion is objectively worse in Los Angeles; it is that the highway building program of the 1950s and 1960s was so successful in reducing congestion that people became used to being able to drive across the entire metropolitan area at a mile a minute, dramatically expanding their choices in living, working, and recreation in the process. Since then, L.A.'s population has grown dramatically, but road building has slowed because of political pressures. This squeeze produced the inevitable result: more congestion.

Some Los Angeles residents now find themselves even more frustrated about traffic than residents of Paris or New York City. This has little to do with the traffic itself, however, and everything to do with the fact that Parisians and New Yorkers never entertained the possibility that they could drive through the center of the city at 60 miles per hour. The problem in Los Angeles is a deflation of greatly raised expectations.

Today's unprecedented concern about sprawl is similarly an indication of how much expectations have risen among ordinary urban dwellers. Metropolitan changes have become such an issue in Los Angeles and Atlanta not because these are inherently undesirable places to live. Quite the contrary. These places have become so attractive that many new residents have flooded in. This has been beneficial for much of the population. These cities have generated enormous numbers of jobs and vast wealth for a tremendous number of people. Of course, as in all other cities throughout history, there have been problems. . . .

Blame the Other Guy

When asked, most Americans declare themselves to be against sprawl, just as they say they are against pollution or the destruction of historic buildings. But the very development that one individual targets as sprawl is often another family's much-loved community. Very few people believe that they themselves live in sprawl, or contribute to sprawl. Sprawl is where other people live, particularly people with less good taste. Much anti-sprawl activism is based on a desire to reform these other people's lives.

Growing numbers of people have discovered that it . . . [moving to the suburbs] is the surest way to obtain the rich, satisfying life all citizens crave.

Affluent exurban residents are among the most zealous guardians of the status quo. They are often adamant about preserving their area exactly as it was when they arrived. Yet rural areas, after a century of losing people as farmers abandoned their land for the cities, are now being repopulated, often at nineteenth-century densities. The new residents are urban families who want the look of old rural New England, but with all of today's urban conveniences. They demand the aesthetic experience of "traditional" settlements without all of the inconveniences associated with that kind of landscape.

This trend, while much accelerated by affluence, has been going on for a long time. Among the best documented inhabitants of exurbia are a number of early American prophets of what we now know as environmentalism. Think of Henry David Thoreau in his shack at Walden Pond just beyond suburban Boston, John Muir in a house across the Berkeley hills from San Francisco, Aldo Leopold at his weekend retreat near Madison, Wisconsin. These were all exurbanites, individuals who loved what they considered a rural life but who also wanted ready access to the city.

Many members of cultural elites are not interested in hearing about the benefits of increased choice for the population at large—because they believe that ordinary citizens, given a choice, will usually make the wrong one. Yet sprawl has certainly increased choices for ordinary citizens.

The indictments against sprawl almost never target architecture or landscapes acceptable to upper-class taste.

At the turn of the century, it was primarily wealthy families who had multiple options in their living, working, and recreational settings. An affluent New York banker and his family could live in many different communities in the city or its suburbs. They could summer in the Adirondacks or at Newport, winter in Florida or on the French Riviera. They had the luxury of ignoring their neighbors and choosing their friends elsewhere.

Today, even the most humble American middle-class family enjoys many of these choices. The privacy, mobility, and freedom that once were available only to the wealthiest and most powerful members of society are now widespread. So if the question is, "Why has sprawl persisted over so many centuries and accelerated in the modern era?" the most convincing answer seems to be that growing numbers of people have discovered that it is the surest way to obtain the rich, satisfying life all citizens crave.

Class Bias Is the Key

Class-based aesthetic objections to sprawl have always been the most important force motivating critics. It seems that as society becomes richer and the resources devoted to securing basics like food and shelter diminish, aesthetic issues loom larger. Certainly the number of people complaining about the visual impact of sprawl, and the vehemence of their rhetoric, have increased with each successive campaign against it.

In both the U.S. and elsewhere, the driving force behind complaints against sprawl at any period seems to be a set of class-related tastes and assumptions.

There is an obvious class bias in these judgments. The indictments against sprawl almost never target architecture or landscapes acceptable to upper-middle-class taste, no matter how scattered or consuming of land. One doesn't hear complaints about the spectacular British villas, the private gardens of the French Riviera created in the 1920s, or the great country houses built by American industrialists at the turn of the century on northern Long Island or in the Brandywine Valley in Delaware. "Sprawl" means subdivisions and shopping centers for middle- and lower-middle-class families. Today it is notoriously "McMansions"—houses judged by some observer to be excessive in size or stylistic pretension.

In both the U.S. and elsewhere, the driving force behind complaints against sprawl at any period seems to be a set of class-related tastes and assumptions, almost always present but rarely discussed. In the nineteenth century, for instance, London exploded outward as developers threw up mile upon mile of brick terrace houses. The resulting cityscape horrified highbrow British critics of the time, who considered the new districts to be vulgar, cheap, and monotonous. Nevertheless, the houses continued to be built, because so many middle-class inhabitants of central London saw them as a vast step upward for their families. Within the last generation or two, elite opinion finally came around, and today these row houses are widely considered to be the very model of compact urban life.

Similarly, during the 1920s the built-up area of greater London underwent a doubling, creating an outward sprawl at least as great as anything seen in recent America. Much of the growth consisted of rows of semidetached houses. These sturdy homes, like the row houses of the nineteenth century, were deprecated by much of the British cultural elite. But they were highly appreciated by ordinary Londoners. And now, ironically enough, these neighborhoods are considered the antithesis of sprawl, and the homes are being lovingly restored by members of the aesthetic elite of the current generation.

Families who have recently moved to the suburban periphery are often the most vociferous opponents of further development.

If history is any guide, the current revolt of the "sensitive minority" against sprawl will soon seem a quaint product of a bygone era. Highbrow critics loudly castigated the landscape created by "vulgar masses" fed by "greedy speculators" in cookie-cutter postwar American suburbs like Daly City, California. But now that their landscapes have matured and their original plastic-shaded floor lamps have become collectible, many of these vintage neighborhoods have become trendy. In like manner, as hard as it is to imagine today, by the time the landscape around the now-treeless subdivisions of look-alike stucco boxes at the edge of suburban Las Vegas fully matures, these subdivisions will likely be candidates for historic landmark designation. Most urban change, no matter how wrenching for one generation, tends to be the accepted norm of the next, and the cherished heritage of the one after that. . . .

Self-Interest and Fear of Change

Although opponents of sprawl believe they are making rational and disinterested diagnoses of urban problems, their actions usually involve powerful, often unacknowledged, self-interest. The self-interest is clear in the case of the New Yorker who owns a weekend home in the Hamptons and rails against the continuing development of Long Island. In similar fashion, families who have recently moved to the suburban periphery are often the most vociferous opponents of further development of exactly the same kind that created their own house, because that would destroy their views or reduce their access to the countryside beyond their subdivision.

The power of self-interest can also be seen in individuals who press for mass transit yet are very unlikely to use it themselves. They assume someone else will ride, and free up highway space for themselves. Here again, members of the incumbents' club form alliances to protect their advantages, sometimes in unexpected and ephemeral ways....

[Sprawl] has been visible in virtually every major city on the globe where incomes have risen and there has been an active real estate market.

The reality is that, rather than declining, many suburbs are actually becoming increasingly gentrified. One of the most visible aspects of this has been the dramatic rise in the number of teardowns: the replacement of smaller houses with much larger ones. One might have thought that teardowns would be welcomed by anti-sprawl forces because they represent a desire to reuse and revitalize older communities. But many of the same organizations that fight sprawl also want to discourage teardowns, claiming they destroy the character of communities. This suggests that the real target might be less sprawl than change itself....

Sprawl Around the World

Enemies of sprawl often hold up dense European city centers as alternatives. But it's not so much the actual preferences of the inhabitants that make those areas the way they are, as simply the fact that their settlement patterns were fixed generations ago in a way that would be hard to alter now. Though many Europeans still live in small apartments in high-density districts, polls consistently confirm that the vast majority of them, like most people worldwide, would rather live in single-family houses on their own piece of land than in an apartment building.

And now that they are becoming affluent enough to act, Europeans are moving into suburbs in increasing numbers. They are bringing jobs and retail with them. In country after country across Europe, consumers are demanding the convenience of longer store hours, shops closer to where they live, and easier access by automobile. The result is a proliferation of large supermarkets, shopping centers, discount centers, and Big Box retail outlets like Wal-Mart or Target. . . .

Suburbanization has created many problems . . . but, on the whole, it appears to have been very beneficial to most urban dwellers.

This process of rapid dispersal has been visible in virtually every major city on the globe where incomes have risen and there has been an active real estate market—from Boston to Bangkok and from Buenos Aires to Berlin. . . .

Getting What We Wished For

For generations, almost all urbanists who critiqued the ills of the modern city ended up advocating dispersal of tightly packed populations. When that really happened on a large scale, the next generation of planners were horrified. Without a doubt, suburbanization has created many problems, as fast change always does. But, on the whole, it appears to have been very beneficial to most urban dwellers.

It's hard for us today to really grasp the nature of city life a hundred years ago, when millions of urban dwellers were obliged to endure cramped and unsanitary tenements, dangerous traffic, pollution-choked streets, and deadly factories. The cleaner, greener, safer, more private neighborhoods that most metropolitan residents now live in would astound our great-grandparents. At very least, our highly dispersed urban regions deserve a bit of respect, before we jump to the conclusion that they are terrible places in need of total transformation.

Some Criticisms of Urban Sprawl Are Not Supported by Serious Research

Samuel R. Staley and Matthew Hisrich

Samuel R. Staley directs the Quality Growth Initiative for the Buckeye Institute, a nonpartisan research and educational institute devoted to individual liberty, economic freedom, personal responsibility, and limited government in Ohio. Staley also directs the Urban Futures Program at Reason Public Policy Institute in Los Angeles and is the author of the 2001 book, Smarter Growth: Market-based Land-use Strategies for the 21st Century. *Matthew Hisrich is a policy analyst at the Buckeye Institute. This article is based on the report* Urban Sprawl and Quality Growth, *published by the Buckeye Institute.*

Local governments . . . are instituting restrictive growth controls to limit housing development, all in an effort to "control" urban sprawl.

But what is urban "sprawl"? Activist groups often comment on the term with platitudes, but few take the time to define it in a meaningful sense. Even reports on regional growth seem to take the term for granted. Citizens for Civic Renewal in Cincinnati [Ohio], for example, commissioned a study on the region's growth that concludes with the claim its proposals offer a "distinct strategy for dealing with the sprawl problem." The study, however, doesn't explicitly define what urban sprawl is.

The Sierra Club defines sprawl as "irresponsible, poorly planned development that destroys green space, increases traffic, crowds schools and drives up taxes." Yet, this definition is

Samuel R. Staley and Matthew Hisrich, "Restricting Housing Not Answer to Local Growth Problems," Buckeye Institute, January 16, 2002. www.buckeyeinstitute.org. Reproduced by permission.

completely useless as a guide to policy: Almost anything that adds a house, car, or child to a community could be labeled sprawl. Balanced discussion is also virtually nonexistent in these reports and studies. In some cases, this is an intentional attempt to create a sense of crisis to spur support for growth controls.

Growth Control Not Based on Sound Analysis

Not surprisingly, while defining "urban sprawl" is an apparent inconvenience, growth control advocates are usually much more up front about what they want to do: restrict housing choice and population growth through housing moratoria, urban-growth boundaries, large-lot zoning, and farmland preservation ordinances.

Unfortunately, many . . . communities may be jumping the gun in attempting to control growth, basing their efforts more on rhetoric than on sound policy analysis. For example, a national survey of more than 475 studies on sprawl and its effects published by the Transportation Research Board identified 42 costs and benefits of low-density suburban development. General agreement was found on only six issues. Some fit the emerging antisprawl conventional wisdom, but others don't. New suburban development, most researchers seem to agree, increases the number of automobile trips and miles traveled. It also reduces the total amount of agricultural land.

On the other hand, scholars agreed that sprawl reduces congestion and provides important mobility benefits because it encourages the use of the automobile. The car, it turns out, is generally recognized as a quicker, more flexible, and generally more efficient way to get around.

Substantially less agreement was found on other issues such as whether sprawl increased the costs of providing roads, sewers, water and other infrastructure, or whether sprawl fostered racial segregation or threatened transit use.

The sweeping criticism of sprawl appears to be inconsistent with a substantial portion of the serious research.

In Ohio, the argument against suburban development doesn't fare much better. For example:

- Most of the state remains rural in character—just 14% of Ohio's total land area is developed (including rural roads and highways) indicating concerns about the loss of open space are local, not statewide;

- Agricultural productivity has increased steadily since the 1950s despite dramatic declines in the number of farms and amount of land in farms;

- As much farmland is converted to forests, pasture, and range as is developed, and the factors that cause farmland conversion are driven more by the economics of the agricultural industry than the demand for urban land;

- Air quality has improved steadily since the 1970s even though automobile use has skyrocketed;

- Congestion is a significant problem only during selected times of the day. Severe traffic congestion is concentrated in Ohio's three largest cities: Columbus, Cleveland, and Cincinnati.

Thus, the sweeping criticism of sprawl appears to be inconsistent with a substantial portion of the serious research already conducted.

Still, many are legitimately concerned about how their communities can grapple with the effects of new homes and families on congestion, public service costs, schools, and open space. Growth restrictions, though, often have unintended consequences. Limiting the supply of housing tends to raise housing prices, limit housing choice, and shift growth into new areas. Existing residential areas may also face market pressures to develop housing at densities higher than many residents would prefer.

Other Options

Most of these problems associated with growth can be addressed without limiting housing choice. Local citizens in Ohio have already taken the initiative to address some of these issues in their own communities. In Cincinnati, for example, a group of neighbors banned together in an attempt to purchase nearby land they felt was facing development pressure. A neighborhood in Cleveland actually took the step to try and cut off city services such as snow removal and leaf collection, preferring private local control to the possibility of unwanted retail development on their street. 36 local and regional land trusts control almost 24,000 acres in Ohio.

Citizens and policymakers can't ignore the consequences of growth. But they should also recognize the consequences of unduly restricting housing development and ensure that a vibrant, consumer-oriented housing market remains a key goal of their growth-management strategy.

CHAPTER 2

Does Urban Sprawl Harm the Environment?

Chapter Preface

Urban sprawl—the seemingly endless maze of housing developments, highways, and strip malls that ring many cities and communities—is criticized for causing a multitude of problems, including traffic jams, deterioration of the inner cities, destruction of farmland and open spaces, and environmental pollution. Many scientists and environmental advocates say, however, that one of the most serious threats from sprawl is its impact on biodiversity, a term short for biological diversity, which refers to the complex network of diverse plant and animal life that together create and sustain an ecosystem in nature.

Sprawl critics explain that the infringement of housing and businesses on farmlands and rural areas is devouring natural habitats and ecosystems and threatening the survival of indigenous species. Sprawl also brings increased water and air pollution, which further degrades natural environments. Some animals require large hunting grounds or pastures to sustain themselves and reproduce, and the fragmentation of countryside by highways and housing subdivisions cuts into and thus destroys these animal habitats, threatening them with extinction. In addition, numerous birds, plants, and other species are dependent on rivers, ponds, or other water sources that may be redirected, eliminated, or polluted by human development and hard-surface runoff. Moreover, many species, both plants and animals, are dependent on each other, so if one species dies off due to pressure from development, others may be indirectly threatened, too. As Carl Pope, executive director of the environmental group Sierra Club, has written in an article posted on the Property and Environmental Research Center's Web site (www.perc.org/perc.php?id=356), urban sprawl "fragments landscapes—and fragmented landscapes are the biggest threat to America's wildlife heritage."

Studies suggest that sprawl is caused by a number of factors, but two major causes are growing human populations and the tendency for fewer and fewer people to occupy larger and larger homes. As household size diminishes, more homes are needed to house the same number of people, even if population does not increase. But the world's population is increasing sharply, which places even more pressure on the environment.

In highly developed countries such as the United States, this trend has been apparent for many decades. Especially since the end of World War II when the abundance of cheap oil created a booming economy as well as an addiction to automobile transportation, Americans have been deserting the cities to move farther and farther out into surrounding rural areas. Moreover, sprawl is increasing in many developing countries, where it is eating into biodiversity "hotspots"—regions such as tropical rain forests that are rich in natural resources and that contain a concentrated array of plant and animal species.

This sprawl of the human population into some of the last remaining regions of natural landscape, critics say, ultimately hurts humans because people rely on nature to purify the air, enrich the soil, and preserve water; to absorb carbon dioxide emissions; and thus keep the planet livable. The planet's diverse life forms also provide ingredients for various drugs used in medical care. No one knows for certain what the breaking point is, but if critical plant and animal species become extinct, the human population might someday be threatened as well.

From the late twentieth century into the early twenty-first, many scientists began expressing alarm about the rate of biodiversity loss. Between 1997 and 2007, studies appeared that suggested that both plant and animal species are dying at a rate not seen for millions of years. Some researchers predict, for example, that fish and coral reefs will be sharply depleted by the middle of the twenty-first century. Global warming—the increase in the Earth's temperatures caused by carbon emissions from the use of fossil fuels—is a leading cause of this process.

Not everyone, however, is convinced that urban sprawl inevitably causes harm to the environment. Some people argue that the environmental threat is exaggerated, that there is still ample open space and farmland in the United States and other parts of the world. The authors of the viewpoints in this chapter provide a range of perspectives on the relationship between sprawl and habitat loss, pollution, and other environmental threats.

Urban Sprawl Is a Major Environmental Concern

Clean Water Action Council

Clean Water Action Council is a nonprofit citizen organization that works to protect public health and the environment in Northeast Wisconsin.

Land use and urban sprawl are major environmental concerns affecting us in a variety of ways. We must adopt sustainable patterns of development which are not self-destructive.

"Sprawl" is the increased use of urbanized land by fewer people than in the past. Traditional cities were compact and efficient, but over the past 30–50 years, the density of land used per person has declined drastically. Although the U.S. population grew by 17 percent from 1982 to 1997, urbanized land increased by 47 percent during the same 15 year period. The developed acreage per person has nearly doubled in the past 20 years, and housing lots larger than 10 acres have accounted for 55 percent of land developed since 1994, according to the American Farmland Trust.

Impacts of Sprawl

1. *Loss of Farmland*——We're chewing up farms at an alarming rate across the U.S., to create new highways, fringe industrial parks and sprawled housing developments. This loss reduces our ability to grow food, fiber and timber. In many areas, urban development pressure and increased property taxes are forcing farmers out of business. They often sell their farms for housing developments, to provide financial security for their retirement. . . .

Clean Water Action Council, "Land Use & Urban Sprawl," www.cwac.net, July 24, 2007. Reproduced by permission.

Nationwide—more than 13.7 million acres of farmland in the U.S. were converted to non-farm use just between 1992 and 1997, according to United States Department of Agriculture. This figure is 51% higher than between 1982 and 1992.

Wild forests, meadows, and wetlands are also disappearing, replaced by pavement, buildings and sterile urban landscaping.

---

2. *Loss of Wildlife Habitat*——Wild forests, meadows, and wetlands are also disappearing, replaced by pavement, buildings and sterile urban landscaping. The remaining habitat is smaller, degraded and more fragmented, making survival of certain wildlife species very difficult as they try to reach breeding ponds, hibernation sites, feeding locations, or to establish viable nesting areas. According to the Wisconsin Department of Natural Resources, [for example] important habitat types are disappearing. . . .

- *Grasslands*—Wisconsin has only .5% (13,000 acres) of its original grassland ecosystem remaining in a relatively intact condition, but much of this remnant acreage has been degraded to some degree

- *Oak Savannas*—Intact examples of oak savanna vegetation are now so rare that less than 500 acres are listed in the Natural Heritage Inventory as having a plant assemblage similar to the original oak savanna. This is less than 0.01% of the original 5.5 million acres.

- *Oak and Pine Barrens*—Less than 1% of the presettlement oak and pine barren habitat remains

- *Shorelands*—Degradation of near-shore and shoreline wildlife habitat is increasing with the pace of development, particularly in northern Wisconsin where, since 1960, two-thirds of the larger lakes have been developed, the number of home sites has doubled, and the annual number of permits for sea wall construction has tripled. The DNR now reviews and processes over 10,000 permits for piers, near shore ponds, and structures each year.

- *Wetlands*—More than 50% of Wisconsin's original wetlands have been lost. On the lower Bay of Green Bay, more than 90% of the wetlands are gone.

3. Increased Tax Burden——The costs of providing community services have skyrocketed as homes and businesses spread farther and farther apart, and local governments are forced to provide for widely spaced services. Owners of these dispersed developments seldom pay the full government costs of serving them, forcing the rest of us to subsidize them with higher taxes at the local, state and federal level.

Sprawl increases car and truck traffic, leading to major increases in air pollution and smog.

An example: A master plan for the State of New Jersey evaluated conventional sprawl growth patterns against a mix of "infill" development, higher density concentrated new development and traditional sprawl. The projected differences are large. Infill and higher density growth would result in a savings of $1.18 billion in roads, water and sanitary sewer construction (or more than $12,000 per new home) and $400 million in direct annual savings to local governments. Over 15 years, it amounts to $7.8 billion. This does not take into account reductions in the cost of other public infrastructure that result from "infill" growth: decreased spending on storm drainage, less need for school busing (and parent taxi service), fewer fire stations, and less travel time for police, ambulance, garbage collection, and other services.

4. *Increased Air Pollution*——Sprawl increases car and truck traffic, leading to major increases in air pollution and smog. Vehicles are the #1 cause of air pollution in many urban areas, and a threat to public and wildlife health.

5. *Increased Water Use and Pollution*——Sprawl increases air pollution, which falls out to become water pollution. In addition, urban activities create water pollution directly, through land runoff of construction site erosion, fuel spills, oil leaks, paint spills, lawn chemicals, pet wastes, etc. Sprawled, low-density development produces more than its share of this runoff. In addition, more water is consumed for lawn watering and other landscape activities, straining local water supply systems.

6. *Increased Energy Consumption*—At a time when we desperately need to reduce our energy use, sprawled developments increase our energy consumption per person, for increased gasoline, home heating, and electricity use.

7. *Social Fragmentation*——Old-fashioned neighborhoods with compact housing, front porches, a corner store, and a school two blocks away were much more conducive to social interactions. It was possible to feel a sense of belonging and community. Now, in sprawled generic housing tracts, many people never meet their neighbors as they pass them in their cars. It's rare for neighborhood events to occur. Families are more isolated and those living alone are marooned in a hostile environment.

8. *Loss of Time*——People are forced to spend more time commuting longer distances to reach their jobs, homes, schools and shopping areas. In a compact, efficient city these travel times are often minimal, but sprawled cities take time to navigate. Suburban tract and country dwellers also spend more time maintaining large, empty residential properties: mowing the grass, plowing long driveways, raking leaves, weeding, etc.

9. *Increased Private Costs and Risks*——Sprawling business and homeowners often fail to realize the long-term personal

costs and risks of maintaining distant properties. As property taxes rise to cover service costs, and fuel costs increase for travel and heating large buildings, the owners' budgets may have trouble keeping up. Transportation costs for children and handicapped family members are much greater. As sprawled homeowners age, their large properties become a greater burden to maintain. When they can no longer drive their car, they are stranded. As baby boomers age, large numbers of people will be forced to sell their suburban or country homes to move into the city, creating displacements and possibly lowering the value of expensive homes.

Experts in the building industry indicate cost differences of $5,000 to $20,000 per dwelling are seen for compact developments with 15 to 25 units per acre versus sprawled developments with only five houses per acre. These are overhead and maintenance costs faced by families, beyond the cost of buying or building the home.

10. *Loss of Exercise*——Sprawled communities force people to drive their cars if they need to get groceries, go to school, or get to work. In the past, cities were structured so many of these destinations were within walking distance. Now, many neighborhoods lack even sidewalks for pedestrians, forcing residents to walk in the street next to the traffic whizzing by. In the past it was normal for kids to walk to school, but now their parents often drive them or they take their own cars. Is it any wonder that an epidemic of obesity is plaguing our country? Walking is the best form of life-long exercise, yet our development patterns actively discourage walking.

11. *Degraded, Noisy Surroundings*——Helter-skelter sprawl is not attractive, yet many of our transportation corridors are now edged with jumbles of residential, commercial, and industrial developments (and their enormous parking lots), which have no sense of beauty or order. This adds to the stressful, disconnected feelings which urban residents often express. We're losing the "green space" we need as part of our

natural heritage. Large areas of noisy, speeding traffic are also not conducive to peaceful communities. Many people want to live in the country to escape this stress, but urban escapees are helping to create these problems instead, as they commute back to the city for work, school and shopping.

12. *Tourism Industry Damage*——As human developments sprawl into the countryside and wildlife habitat shrinks, we're rapidly losing the scenic qualities that attract tourists to our region. Our country roads are being straightened and widened, or worse yet, converted into 4 lane highways (often with additional frontage roads and ugly billboards). Hunters are left with fewer and smaller hunting lands. Anglers are left with crowded, less-appealing fishing sites. This will have direct economic impacts . . . [for tourism].

There Is a Clear Connection Between Urban Sprawl and Air Pollution

Matt Weiser

Matt Weiser is a staff writer for the Bakersfield Californian *newspaper. He won a first place award in the 2004 American Planning Association Journalism Award Competition for his 2003 newspaper series on air pollution in Bakersfield.*

Urban sprawl has been blamed for many things, but air pollution isn't always one of them. Usually it's loss of farmland, blighted downtowns, and longer commutes that drive the smart growth agenda. But in Bakersfield, California, residents are reluctantly waking up to the need for a new approach to urban planning that minimizes air pollution. Last year the American Lung Association ranked Bakersfield as having the third-worst air quality in the nation. The city is part of the federally designated San Joaquin Valley air basin, the largest in the nation and the one with the second-worst air quality in the U.S., behind only the notoriously smog-blurred Los Angeles region. Compounding the problem, Bakersfield is also considered a poster child for sprawl. A Brookings Institution study in 2001 ranked it as the most sprawling city in California, and the fourth worst in the U.S.

A Lack of Land Use Standards

The region is blessed with an abundance of affordable land and a dependable water supply, unlike many areas of California. And with double-digit unemployment straining the region for decades, politicians have been reluctant to impose new development standards, fearing they would harm the construction industry.

So, until now, there have been few incentives for smart growth in Bakersfield (pop. 266,000), California's 12th largest city. Local development codes contain no requirements for compact growth, mixed-use development, or even pedestrian-friendly neighborhood design. The typical new Bakersfield housing subdivision is a network of looping streets and cul de sacs, with high sound walls sealing off each neighborhood from the next. Local leaders have found little reason to change this pattern, and they continue to question planning's role in improving air quality. "There's no science that says the way projects look on the ground would reduce emissions," says Stanley Grady, planning director for the city of Bakersfield. "Urban design, by itself, is not what's going to improve air quality."

The biggest change on the horizon is a new development fee intended to offset growth's impact on air quality . . . [—] an "indirect source rule."

Change Is Coming

Yet the public is clamoring for action as they suffer the city's brown skies and rising rates of asthma and other smog-related health problems. And, in fact, several small steps are being taken along the road to lung-friendly urban planning. Among those steps:

- The local Sierra Club chapter has filed successful legal challenges against several Bakersfield residential developments to protest their impact on air quality. The club has agreed to settle each case in return for a payment by the developer of $1,200 per home. An appointed board, representing all parties, will spend the money on other pollution control projects, such as regional bike paths and clean-fuel engine conversions.

- To avoid more such lawsuits, both the city and Kern County, which jointly administer the Metro Bakersfield general plan, are working with developers to adopt additional residential pollution controls.

Until now, a subdivision has escaped scrutiny if computer models showed it would generate no more than 10 tons of air pollution annually, an amount considered "significant" by the San Joaquin Valley Air Pollution Control District, the state agency that regulates regional air quality. Now, city and county planners are working with residential developers to mitigate each project's emissions down to zero. The new strategy relies on a menu of pollution control projects that includes documented emission reductions.

In one recent [as of 2004] proposal to build 412 homes on quarter-acre lots, studies showed the project would cause 19 tons per year of air pollution. To achieve an equal amount of pollution reduction, the developer agreed to crush older model cars, contribute money toward the purchase of new low-emission public fleet vehicles, and replace stationary diesel engines, such as those used in agriculture, with cleaner burning models. "We're quantifying specific measures that a project proponent has to do that improve air quality," says Ted James, AICP, Kern County planning director. "The important things are that we give applicants a choice and that there is a measurable benefit."

For the first time ever, city and county leaders last year also adopted a tiered transportation impact fee designed to encourage infill development. The fee as originally adopted in 1991 charged developers $1,179 per home to cover a project's impacts on the regional road network. The fee has been increased in small increments since then, reaching $2,466 in early 2003. Last year, the city and county increased the fee to $2,882 in a designated core area of Bakersfield, and $5,813 elsewhere in town. It is hoped this tiered fee will discourage sprawl by making development on the edges of town more expensive.

Last Resort: Pay to Pollute?

The biggest change on the horizon is a new development fee intended to offset growth's impact on air quality. Called an "indirect source rule," it would give developers a choice between paying a fee to offset the pollution their projects cause, changing their projects to reduce air pollution, or some combination of both. Every project, commercial and residential, would be required to correct a fixed percentage of its emissions. That percentage has not been decided yet. Proposed by the valley air district, the indirect source rule would be the largest application of this concept ever in the nation.

[California's San Joaquin] valley's primary summer pollution problem is ground-level ozone . . . [caused by] vehicle exhaust.

Builders could adopt onsite improvements such as additional tree canopy, easy access to public transit, and energy efficiency measures. They could also get credit for locating close to the center of town, mixing commercial and residential development, and building at higher densities. If such onsite changes did not offset enough pollution, the developer would pay a fee to atone for the rest. Fees collected under the rule would then be spent on other air-quality projects, such as consumer rebates for low polluting lawnmowers, building telecommuting sites, or subsidizing public transit. "We'd like to think this is an incentive to grow smart and not have leapfrog development," says Jennifer Barba, a planner and air quality specialist charged with developing the rule for the valley air district. "But some might see it as a pay-to-pollute situation. It just depends on what the developer chooses to do. We're just trying to push it along."

The rule . . . was tried once before, in the early 1990s, but was crushed by opposition from developers. Now there are new imperatives: The rule is already factored into emission reductions in the valley's federally approved plan to control particulate pollution, and a new state law, SB 709, sponsored by Sen. Dean Florez (D-Shatter), specifically requires the district to adopt an indirect source rule. The air district has no direct legal authority over mobile sources (cars and trucks) or urban planning decisions. So the indirect source rule is one of the few tools for addressing the rising problem of growth-related air pollution.

"There's a significant amount of growth occurring in the entire basin, and that growth is offsetting some of the reductions we're getting from stationary sources, or traditional sources," says Barba. "In the minds of the general public it seems to be, not out of control, but growing rapidly."

Air Pollution Is Everywhere

The valley's primary summer pollution problem is ground-level ozone, formed when hydrocarbon and nitrogen oxide emissions combine in the presence of sunlight. In the San Joaquin Valley, vehicle exhaust causes two-thirds of these emissions. Ozone is natural and desirable in the atmosphere's highest altitudes, where it helps shield the planet from harmful ultraviolet radiation. But at ground level, it destroys lung tissue and hinders crop and forest growth.

In winter, the primary culprit is particulate pollution caused by combustion. Among the biggest sources are wood-burning for home heating and the open burning of crop waste on farms. Particulates contribute to smog formation, but also cause a wide range of health problems, including asthma, bronchitis, and heart disease.

Last year, with support from the Building Industry Association, the valley air district passed a rule that bans heating with wood during episodes of poor air quality, and requires older woodstoves to be removed when existing homes are sold. It also strictly limits the number of fireplaces allowed in new development.

In the San Joaquin Valley, planning for air quality is especially important, because the region is burdened by a combination of topography and weather that makes air pollution worse. The valley, one of America's most productive farming regions, is surrounded on three sides by mountains. The north end is open to prevailing winds, which blow air pollution from north to south. Bakersfield sits at the south end of the valley. Here, pollutants pile up against surrounding mountains and stagnate. In the summer, continuous sunlight and temperatures that regularly top 100 degrees create a perfect menu for cooking emissions into harmful smog. In winter, temperature inversion layers cause the valley's infamous tule fog and trap pollutants at ground level. Both in winter and summer, winds are usually light, preventing dispersion.

Sprawl makes air pollution worse by focusing growth at the edges of cities, forcing people to drive farther to reach work and shopping. It puts more cars on the road for short trips, increases idling time at congested intersections, and limits opportunities for walking, biking, and public transit. Vehicles also cause particulate pollution from brake and the wear, and by stirring up road dust. These sources are largely unregulated, and difficult to control. Experts have proved that the more cars you have in a community, and the more they are driven, the more particulates end up in the air people breathe.

Then there are consumer products that come along with new housing. Every lawnmower, barbecue, motorcycle, and can of paint becomes part of the problem. Many of these fall into a polluter category called "areawide sources." These are expected to increase with population growth. Some can be contained via smart growth development, some cannot.

Growth-related pollution also comes from the commercial development that inevitably accompanies new housing. Every new gas station, dry cleaner, auto repair shop, and restaurant represents a small but incremental increase in air pollution.

Many of these are regulated as "stationary sources." Other cities have used their planning authority to ban or restrict obvious polluters in this category, such as drive-through restaurants and banks. Bakersfield has not taken this step. . . .

More Sprawl Ahead?

Other communities in the San Joaquin Valley have recognized the connection between sprawl and smog. In 2001, for instance, Fresno County's government, farming, and development leaders formed a partnership to fight sprawl. Known as the Fresno Growth Alternatives Alliance, the group produced a set of smart growth standards later adopted by county leaders and every city in the county. The standards, dubbed "A Landscape of Choice," call for narrower streets, greater densities, more infill development, and transit-friendly planning, among other things. And in 2002 the city of Lemoore (pop. 21,000), in Kings County, took a bold step by imposing smart growth development standards on all vacant land. The new rules require narrower grid-patterned streets, varied architecture, shorter building setbacks, a thicker tree canopy, and a variety of traffic-calming measures.

Founded in 1873, Bakersfield already has a model of infill development right within its oldest neighborhoods. Clustered around the original downtown, these neighborhoods have the very features that nearby communities are trying to impose. However, the present growth pattern requires different uses to be separated, and local leaders are reluctant to revive the older standards today. "You have to modify your development standards to support that kind of land-use planning," says Grady. "You'd actually have to require people to build differently than they're doing now. There's no science that shows that because you put trees on the street that people aren't going to drive their cars."

Instead, local officials favor incentives to encourage alternative construction modes. James notes that county zoning ordinances encourage mixed use, for example, but he could not recall a single mixed-use project being built as a result. "Some would say that it's the local government's job to mandate that, to make it happen. To me, that's not the way it happens," says James. "Mandates turn people away. We need to be approaching this in a proactive way by creating incentives. We need to create the environment so innovative solutions can come along."

City and county officials are watching warily as the air district's indirect source rule moves forward. They're afraid it will add excessive red tape to the development process, and they want to ensure that any emission reductions claimed under the rule are real and measurable. They also want a guarantee that fees generated by local development under the rule are spent locally.

Controversial though it is, the rule has one limitation: Local zoning may limit which onsite measures developers can adopt to avoid paying the impact fee. For instance, Bakersfield zoning does not allow mixed-use development except by special exemption. If it's not there for builders to choose, in other words, they may simply pay the fee and sprawl will continue. "Air-quality issues are very much integrated with land-use planning issues," says James. "We need to make sure development is compact and contiguous with other development. But are we at a point where we need to stop growth? No. Are we still facilitating sprawl? Well, that's the argument, I guess."

Urban Sprawl Threatens the Nation's Water Supplies

Brian Johnson

Brian Johnson is a writer for the Finance and Commerce Daily Newspaper, *a business newspaper covering Minneapolis and St. Paul, Minnesota.*

Three environmental groups are blaming urban sprawl for contributing to severe water shortages nationally, but a home-building organization says the accusations are unfounded.

Sprawl and Groundwater

A report released in August [2002] by American Rivers, the Natural Resources Defense Council and Smart Growth America concludes that urban development is worsening the nation's water supply problems by sending rainwater into streams and rivers as polluted runoff. Water in less developed regions—which have fewer parking lots, driveways and other hard surfaces—is absorbed into the soil where it replenishes groundwater, according to the report, "Paving the Way to Water Shortages: How Sprawl Aggravates Drought."

The report, which comes at a time [2002] when 49 percent of the country is experiencing either moderate or extreme drought, added that 40 percent of Americans get their water directly from underground sources.

Betsy Otto, senior director for watershed programs at American Rivers, said urban sprawl is literally sending billions of gallons of badly needed water down the drain each year. "We've all become, unfortunately, familiar with the traffic congestion, overcrowded schools, loss of open space and escalating taxes that come along with sprawl development," Otto said. "What I think has been relatively missing in the discussion is, 'What are we doing to our water supplies?'"

Otto likened grasslands, farm fields and other natural surfaces to a giant sponge that draws rainwater into the ground, where it can replenish drinking water aquifers, lakes and rivers. "Rivers on average get 50 percent of their flow from groundwater," she said. "If we interrupt that . . . we've completely changed the natural water cycle." Otto said it's been known for a long time that replacing natural ground with hard surfaces changes the natural water cycle. The goal of the report, which draws from the U.S. Geological Survey and other existing data, is to get a "sense of magnitude" of the problem, she said.

Twin Cities Among Biggest Land Consumers

The report, which examined new land development from 1982 to 1997 in 312 metro areas, ranked the Twin Cities [Minneapolis and St. Paul, MN] as the nation's sixth biggest consumer of land during the study period. Atlanta, Boston, Washington, D.C., Dallas and Houston were the top five.

Builders are becoming more open to environmentally friendly practices.

According to the report, new development in the Twin Cities increased 62 percent from 1982 to 1997. During that time, 286,100 acres were developed in the metro area while the population increased 26 percent. The report also estimated how much groundwater was "lost" to sprawl each year. Because of development, the Twin Cities lost between 9 billion and 21.1 billion gallons of groundwater annually during the study years, according to the report.

In order to mitigate the effects of development, the report urges communities to adopt "smart growth" techniques such as revitalizing existing population centers, providing more transportation choices and protecting open space.

Builders Disagree with Findings

The National Association of Home Builders (NAHB) agrees that communities should consider adopting some of those policies, but disagrees with other findings in the report.

Michael Luzier, senior vice president of regulatory affairs for the NAHB, said it was a stretch to link development with rainfall and drought. "It seems to me that it was an obvious attempt to capitalize on the drought situation," he said. "This implication that ... if we sprawl we will necessarily end up with less water, I think the logic begins to fall apart when you look at it."

Luzier questioned the report's theory that groundwater is lost because of development. Stormwater runoff is typically captured by reservoirs that supply many of the nation's cities, according to NAHB officials. "Whether it gets there through base flow, through groundwater or surface water runoff really doesn't matter to the reservoir," Luzier said. "So any water that were to run off from urbanization, into a body of water, would be there for consumption."

NAHB officials also argue that builders and developers routinely practice environmentally friendly construction techniques, such as building narrower streets with less impervious surface, compact development and stormwater retention ponds. Moreover, despite the rise in development cited in the report, 97 percent of U.S. land remains undeveloped, NAHB officials noted. "We certainly are an advocate of smart growth and a wide range of housing choices," Luzier said. "But there are trade-offs. You pursue one objective at the cost of another, and that's always the case. It's a complicated system out there."

Otto agreed that builders are becoming more open to environmentally friendly practices. "In terms of techniques to reduce imperviousness, and to capture and infiltrate stormwater on site, we are starting to see more of that being done," she said. "That's great. It needs to be more common."

Urban Sprawl Is Threatening Some of the Most Endangered Wildlife

Eddie Nickens

Eddie Nickens is a North Carolina writer and a frequent contributor to National Wildlife, *a magazine published by the National Wildlife Federation, an organization that seeks to protect American wildlife.*

A narrow game trail coursed through saw palmetto, hugging the edge of a swamp deep in Florida's Big Cypress National Preserve. I followed the faint path, eyes on the ground. Shin-high cypress trees snagged my boots. Mosquitoes buzzed my ears. The trail skirted a hammock of soaring cabbage palms, their fronds rattling in a dry November breeze. Just a few hours earlier, a Florida panther had walked this path. I'd seen its tracks from a jeep traversing this muck of pine flatwoods and cypress stands. Scrambling off the vehicle, two biologists and I plunged into the dense woods, picked up the panther's trail through towering live oaks, and tracked it back to the trail crossing.

At the edge of the trail, in a thicket of wax myrtle and red bay, the big predator had stopped, sinking its front paws deep into black mud. Something had caught the cat's eye—the left edges of the tracks were pushed slightly deeper into the soil, as if it had leaned in that direction, raising a tawny muzzle. Perhaps the panther had caught wind of a deer, a primary prey animal, or glimpsed an armadillo scuffling through the briars. I couldn't tell. But this much I did know: There are roughly 60 adult Florida panthers remaining in the world, and one of these magnificent felines had been standing right here, sifting the air for scent, pondering its next move.

In the three-quarter-million-acre Big Cypress preserve, that panther had plenty of options. Not so its kin in the surrounding region. Rich upland forests to the north and west are ideal habitat for the big cats, but they also are home to one of the nation's fastest-growing human populations. Kneeling beside the fist-sized panther tracks we'd discovered, Kris Thoemke, a biologist for the National Wildlife Federation's Everglades Project Office, sounded a rueful note. "This is wild country," he said, "but it's also the front line for the battle over urban sprawl and wildlife habitat."

Wide-ranging animals . . . find themselves hemmed in by roads, golf courses and new neighborhoods.

Long cited for its pernicious effects on the quality of human life, from increased traffic to air and water pollution, urban sprawl is also putting the squeeze on wildlife as diverse as panthers, bears, birds, fish and mussels. From the outskirts of Naples here in Florida to the growing footprints of major cities in Georgia, California, Arizona and beyond, ever-expanding suburbs are gobbling up millions of acres of wildlife habitat every year. Local officials have begun to grapple with solutions to the problem, but it's still too soon to predict whether relief will come in time for the most vulnerable species.

Sprawl's impact on wildlife goes beyond the obvious. More roads and cars spawn air and even water pollution (when gas and oil run off roadways into streams). Land clearing also loads streams with sediment, which smothers fish eggs and bottom-dwelling invertebrates and chokes out streamside food and cover plants. And simplified suburban landscapes give exotic and weedy competitors an edge over natives. Even if patches of land are left undeveloped, sprawling growth, often ever-expanding suburbs, are gobbling up millions of acres of wildlife habitat every year. Wide-ranging animals, meanwhile, which need large, contiguous blocks of wild or semi-wild landscape, find themselves hemmed in by roads, golf courses and new neighborhoods.

The Florida Panther Example

That's the case with Felis concolor coryi, the Florida panther. A subspecies of North American mountain lion, Florida panthers can be identified by three distinctive physical features: a right-angle crook near the end of the tail; irregular white speckling on the head, neck and shoulders; and a cowlick in the middle of the back. The cats are impressive creatures, with mature males growing some seven feet long from nose to the black tip of the tail.

Leapfrog development is one of urban sprawl's more insidious characteristics.

Preying mostly on white-tailed deer, Florida panthers are solitary hunters, and the cats need space. The home range of male panthers averages about 185 square miles, and an individual might roam 20 miles during a single day. In the past, the animals ranged from the southern tip of Florida north to South Carolina and west to Texas, but—after being overhunted until 1958—they are being crowded out by human development. Today [2001] the only remaining population is in southwest Florida, where new highways, condominium complexes and golf-course communities threaten the cat's survival.

It's easy to see what's happening to prime Florida panther habitat. Forty miles west of those pawprints in the mud sits Naples, the seat of Collier County and the nation's most active new residential construction market. The county's population grew from 86,000 in 1980 to 227,000 in 2000, and it is projected to double again in the next three decades. According to NWF [National Wildlife Fund], attorney John Kostyack, state and federal authorities have approved the destruction of 6,000 acres of panther habitat since 1993, with at least 29,000 additional acres under threat of development.

One morning I crisscrossed the cat's last stronghold by car. Leaving downtown Naples, I drove north, through miles of sprawling shopping centers and gated golf-course developments. As the occupied neighborhoods petered out, new developments under construction appeared as huge holes bulldozed out of the forest. Halfway to Fort Myers, I passed through a moonscape of bare earth several miles in extent. It turned out to be buildings that would support the new Florida Gulf Coast University—touted as a center for environmentally oriented programs—which is being carved out of cypress woods and palmetto groves known to harbor panthers. Farther east into the countryside, "for sale" signs whizzed by the window—130-, 320-, 670- and 1,006-acre projects.

Such leapfrog development is one of urban sprawl's more insidious characteristics, and Florida by no means has cornered the market. According to the Natural Resources Defense Council (NRDC), suburban populations have grown ten times faster than urban ones in the country's largest metropolitan areas since 1980. In Maryland, more open space will be converted to housing between 1995 and 2020 than during the last 350 years. Phoenix is developing 1.2 acres of land every hour. And the suburbs of Atlanta now sprawl for a linear distance of 110 miles. Still, there's no end in sight: The U.S. population is expected to grow by half over the next 50 years. That's the equivalent of adding all the residents of today's Germany and France, note the authors of an NRDC book, *Once There Were Greenfields,* that outlines the perils of sprawl.

Wildlife Threatened in Other Locations

The Florida panther may be one of sprawl's more charismatic casualties, but it is by no means alone. In Arizona, for example, the seven-inch cactus ferruginous pygmy owl is threatened by ever-spreading suburbs. A recent U.S. Fish and Wildlife Service survey located fewer than 35 adult owls throughout the entire state, and all but two were found in Tucson's rapidly growing Pima County, where human population has increased from 400,000 in the early 1970s to nearly 850,000 today [2001].

In the Southeast, a hand-sized freshwater mussel called the Carolina heelsplitter was once found in streams throughout the Piedmont region of the Carolinas. Today the mussel, a federally listed endangered species, is found in only six creeks, and each of them lies directly in the path of sprawling Charlotte, North Carolina. New driveways, rooftops, streets and gutters there have worsened storm-water runoff, which in turn scours creek banks, silts up clear streams and washes mussels into poorer downstream habitat. According to John Alderman, a wildlife biologist with the North Carolina Wildlife Resources Commission, all six remaining heelsplitter populations are significantly threatened by Charlotte's expansion. "If you're an aquatic species," he says, "this is not a very pleasant place to live."

Enumerating solutions to urban sprawl is far easier than putting them into practice.

Nor is sprawling Seattle for endangered chinook salmon. Migrating from Puget Sound up the region's rivers to spawn, these fish run the gauntlet of Seattle's exploding megapolis, especially those that swim the Cedar River. While upstream stretches of the river include some of the area's highest-quality aquatic habitat, sprawl is threatening to siphon off more and more of its water. A recently approved [as of 2001] plan negotiated by city, state and federal officials guarantees Seattle's burgeoning population more than 100 million gallons of Cedar River water each day, and fishery managers are worried that there soon may not be enough left over for the fish. Already, 22 of 25 stocks of Puget Sound salmon fail to meet U.S. Fish and Wildlife Service spawning goals for the species.

In Southern California's San Diego County, so many wildlife species are threatened by sprawl that it's difficult to hold up just one example; the county is home to more endangered species than any other in the contiguous United States. Sprawl's victims include populations of the California gnatcatcher, arroyo toad, fairy shrimp and peninsular bighorn sheep—all listed by the federal government as either threatened or endangered. Particularly hard hit are coastal sage-scrub habitats—important to a wealth of wildlife species— which have declined some 60 percent since 1945. Inked in 1998, a multi-agency conservation strategy for 85 imperiled species is lauded for targeting 171,920 acres of habitat for protection in San Diego County, but conservationists worry there will not be enough money for acquiring, monitoring and managing the protected lands.

Smart Growth and Other Solutions

Indeed, enumerating solutions to urban sprawl is far easier than putting them into practice. Yet change is possible. Most ideas are bundled loosely within a platform of "smart growth" policies intended to prompt cities and towns to plan neighborhoods that mix offices, shops and homes and make work and play accessible by foot, bicycle or public transit.

Instead of encouraging sprawl into rural areas through large road-building projects, for example, municipalities are persuaded to "infill," or direct new growth to already settled areas. Urban growth boundaries, which stimulate growth inside a prescribed boundary, make it more attractive for developers to build inside an urban core than at its rural fringe, drawing a line in the woods or desert or prairie beyond which sprawl is curtailed. Despite technical problems and some entrenched resistance to such changes, there now are enough smart-growth success stories to suggest that urban sprawl is not necessarily the way life has to be.

Consider Portland. Like all Oregon cities, it was required by state law in 1973 to draw an urban-growth boundary around its metropolitan core and to discourage dense development outside the line. But Portland went even further, enacting the Metro 2040 Growth Concept, a municipal document outlining how, and where, the region plans to grow into the middle of the twenty-first century. Specifically, Metro 2040 promotes the development of mixed-use centers: communities that offer employment, housing, retail shops and both cultural and recreational amenities in a walkable environment serviced by public transit. Already, mass transit use in Portland is increasing at a faster rate than automobile use, and the Metro 2040 concept, when fully implemented, will cut road construction by 25 percent and save 100,000 acres from development. All this, and the plan still makes room for 720,000 new residents.

Just outside Washington, D.C., Maryland's Montgomery County tried a different approach to curbing sprawl: a program that helps stave off the conversion of farmlands to residential subdivisions. Under the plan, launched two decades ago, property owners within a designated agricultural-reserve area are allowed to sell a parcel's development rights to another party—such as a developer or real estate investor—and those rights are then transferred to a land parcel within an urban area. Known as a "transfer of development rights" (TDR) program, the swapping scheme leaves farmlands as open space while generating income for landowners. To date, 41,270 acres of land have been saved through the program—prompting the *Washington Post* to dub Montgomery County "the land that suburban sprawl forgot."

Many Challenges

Still, cities seeking to curb sprawl face many challenges, and South Florida's attempts to grow smarter show just how difficult the effort can be. Collier County, for example, is under a state-imposed moratorium on new building permits, handed down in 1999 when its growth-management plan was deemed unsuitable by state officials. Though the county has since set up an urban boundary, large-scale developments were allowed to move forward just outside it, prompting protests from the Florida Wildlife Federation and other conservation groups. Two years ago, county natural resource managers proposed a TDR program as well as a zoning effort to preserve farmlands, but county commissioners rejected both ideas.

Yet planning advocates say such resistance to curbing sprawl represents little more than the growing pains of an effort to instill into the public mind a whole new way of thinking about development. NRDC senior attorney F. Kaid Benfield, co-author of *Once There Were Greenfields*, points out that we've spent many decades creating today's sprawling suburbs, yet just a few years talking about solutions. "I'm encouraged that there's so much more interest in this issue than there was five years ago," he says.

But will changes come in time to save species like the Florida panther? The day after I tracked that big cat through live oaks and cabbage palms, I took a walk on the beach in downtown Naples. Looking north, the Gulf Coast curved into infinity, a shore crowded with condominiums, homes and high-rises, like polished, close-set teeth, for as far as I could see. The region's rabid development began on this thin fringe of beach, and from here the growth spread inland, where it now has a life of its own, an appetite made greater with each new gated golf-course community. The sand was fine and white, and in the soft beach my hiking boots left clear big impressions. I thought of those panther prints in the Big Cypress mud, where the cat stood in the underbrush, sweeping the trail for signs of prey and hints of danger. Stepping out from the protective scrim of scrub, the panther crossed a muddy wash crisscrossed with alligator tracks, then padded quietly towards a hammock of high ground. For the moment, all seemed well and safe.

Urban Sprawl Is Contributing to Global Warming

Worldwatch Institute

The Worldwatch Institute is a nonpartisan research organization that seeks to provide information and ideas needed to foster a sustainable world.

If governments do not act quickly to discourage the building of cities for cars, the international effort to control global warming will become much more difficult, reports a new study by the Worldwatch Institute, a Washington, D.C.-based research organization. Sprawling urban areas are helping to make road transportation the fastest growing source of the carbon emissions warming the earth's atmosphere.

"Wind turbines, energy-efficient cars, and other new technologies have received much attention in recent debates over energy policy, but we've been neglecting the role that urban design can play in stabilizing the climate," said Molly O'Meara Sheehan, author of *City Limits: Putting the Brakes on Sprawl.* "Local concerns like clogged roads, dirty air, and deteriorating neighborhoods are already fueling a backlash against sprawl. Understanding the role of sprawl in climate change should only speed up the shift towards more parks and less parking lots. We can have healthier, more livable cities and protect the planet from climate change too."

A large body of research shows that sprawl already wreaks havoc on people's health. Each year, traffic accidents take up to a million lives worldwide. In some countries, the number of lives cut short by illness from air pollution exceeds those lost to accidents. And by making driving necessary and walking and cycling less practical, sprawling cities widen waistlines by depriving people of needed exercise.

Worldwatch Institute, "Curbing Sprawl to Fight Climate Change," news release, June 28, 2002. www.worldwatch.org. Reproduced by permission.

Sprawl in the United States

Cities in the United States have been sprawling for decades, spreading out much faster than population growth. Chicago, for example, saw a 38 percent increase in population from 1950 to 1990, but the city's land area grew more than three times as fast, a 124 percent increase.

But U.S. citizens are increasingly dissatisfied with sprawl. A recent national poll found that sprawl topped the list of local concerns. And in the year 2000 election, U.S. voters approved some 400 local and state ballot initiatives addressing sprawl-related problems. At least 38 U.S. states have passed laws creating incentives for more compact development.

The urban design decisions made today, especially in cities in the developing world . . . , will have an enormous impact on global warming.

"The United States has the world's most car-reliant cities," said Sheehan. "U.S. drivers consume roughly 43 percent of the world's gasoline to propel less than 5 percent of the world's population. The big question facing the United States today is whether we can turn away from a car-centered model and develop better land-use practices and less destructive transportation systems."

Curbing Sprawl Around the Globe

By the end of the decade, the majority of the world's people will live in urban areas. The urban design decisions made today [2002], especially in cities in the developing world where car use is still low, will have an enormous impact on global warming in the decades ahead. Adoption of the U.S. car-centered model in these places would have disastrous consequences.

Thirty years from now, for example, China, excluding Hong Kong, is expected to have 752 million urban dwellers. If each were to copy the transportation habits of the average resident of the San Francisco area in 1990, the carbon emissions from transportation in urban China alone could exceed 1 billion tons, roughly as much carbon as released in 1998 from all road transportation worldwide.

"Some cities in developing countries have already proved that a strategy of de-emphasizing cars and providing public transit instead can work," said Sheehan. One outstanding example is the city of Curitiba, Brazil. Starting in 1972, Curitiba built a system of dedicated busways and zoned for higher-density development along those thoroughfares—and is now enjoying better air quality and more parks for its 2.5 million people.

Today [2002], other Latin American cities are adapting elements of Curitiba's system. Bogota, Colombia, has recently launched a similar bus system, the *TransMilenio*, expanded its bike paths, and tried a bold "car-free" day, where in the middle of the work week, the city of 6.8 million functioned as normal—but without cars. Bogota's story also illustrates the importance of higher population density to support buses and cycling: if Bogota sprawled like a typical American city, it would cover more than 20 times as much land area.

Another indication of the reaction against sprawl is the growth of light rail and other forms of public transit. A surge in light rail construction has brought the total number of systems in Western Europe to over 100 in 2000, the highest point since 1970. In the United States, public transportation use has increased for five straight years, following decades of decline. Planners in Portland, Oregon, estimate that a new light rail line there has saved the region from building eight new parking garages and two extra lanes on major highways.

Urban Sprawl and Automobiles Cause Fewer Environmental Problems than Many People Think

Ted Balaker and Sam Staley

Ted Balaker and Sam Staley are coauthors of the book The Road More Traveled: Why the Congestion Crisis Matters More than You Think, and What We Can Do About It *(2006).*

They don't rate up there with cancer and al-Qaeda—at least not yet—but suburban sprawl and automobiles are rapidly acquiring a reputation as scourges of modern American society. Sprawl, goes the typical indictment, devours open space, exacerbates global warming and causes pollution, social alienation and even obesity. And cars are the evil co-conspirator—the driving force, so to speak, behind sprawl.

Yet the anti-suburbs culture has also fostered many myths about sprawl and driving, a few of which deserve to be reconsidered.

Americans Are Addicted to Driving

Actually, Americans aren't addicted to their cars any more than office workers are addicted to their computers. Both items are merely tools that allow people to accomplish tasks faster and more conveniently. The New York metropolitan area is home to the nation's most extensive transit system, yet even there it takes transit riders about twice as long as drivers to get to work.

In 1930, the interstate highway system and the rise of suburbia were still decades away, and yet car ownership was already widespread, with three in four households having an automobile. Look at any U.S. city and the car is the dominant mode of travel.

The key factor that affects driving habits isn't population density, public transit availability, gasoline taxes or even different attitudes. It's wealth.

Some claim that Europeans have developed an enlightened alternative. Americans return from London and Paris and tell their friends that everyone gets around by transit. But tourists tend to confine themselves to the central cities. Europeans may enjoy top-notch transit and endure gasoline that costs $5 per gallon, but in fact they don't drive much less than we do. In the United States, automobiles account for about 88 percent of travel. In Europe, the figure is about 78 percent. And Europeans are gaining on us.

The key factor that affects driving habits isn't population density, public transit availability, gasoline taxes or even different attitudes. It's wealth. Europe and the United States are relatively wealthy, but American incomes are 15 to 40 percent higher than those in Western Europe. And as nations such as China and India become wealthier, the portion of their populations that drive cars will grow.

Public Transit Can Reduce Traffic Congestion

Transit has been on the slide for well more than half a century. Even though spending on public transportation has ballooned to more than seven times its 1960s levels, the percentage of people who use it to get to work fell 63 percent from 1960 to 2000 and now stands at just under 5 percent nationwide. Transit is also decreasing in Europe, down to 16 percent in 2000.

Like auto use, suburbanization is driven by wealth. Workers once left the fields to find better lives in the cities. Today more and more have decided that they can do so in the suburbs. Indeed, commuters are now increasingly likely to travel from one suburb to another or embark upon "reverse" commutes (from the city to the suburbs). Also, most American commuters (52 percent) do not go directly to and from work but stop along the way to pick up kids, drop off dry cleaning, buy a latte or complete some other errand.

We have to be realistic about what transit can accomplish. Suppose we could not only reverse transit's long slide but also triple the size of the nation's transit system and fill it with riders. Transportation guru Anthony Downs of the Brookings Institution notes that this enormous feat would be "extremely costly" and, even if it could be done, would not "notably reduce" rush-hour congestion, primarily because transit would continue to account for only a small percentage of commuting trips.

Polls often show that Americans think that air quality is deteriorating. Yet air is getting much cleaner.

But public transit still has an important role. Millions of Americans rely on it as a primary means of transportation. Transit agencies should focus on serving those who need transit the most: the poor and the handicapped. They should also seek out the niches where they can be most useful, such as express bus service for commuters and high-volume local routes.

Many officials say we should reconfigure the landscape— pack people in more tightly—to make it fit better with a transit-oriented lifestyle. But that would mean increasing density in existing developments by bulldozing the low-density neighborhoods that countless families call home. Single-family houses, malls and shops would have to make way for a stacked-up style of living that most don't want. And even then the best-case scenario would be replicating New York, where only one in four commuters uses mass transit.

We Can Cut Air Pollution Only If We Stop Driving

Polls often show that Americans think that air quality is deteriorating. Yet air is getting much cleaner. We miss it because, while we see more people and more cars, we easily overlook the success of air-quality legislation and new technologies. In April 2004, the Environmental Protection Agency reported that 474 counties in 31 states violated the Clean Air Act. But that doesn't mean that the air is dirtier. The widely publicized failing air-quality grades were a result of the EPA's adoption of tougher standards.

One need only take a cross-country flight and look down ... to realize that our nation is mostly open space.

Air quality has been improving for a long time. More stringent regulations and better technology have allowed us to achieve what was previously unthinkable: driving more and getting cleaner. Since 1970, driving—total vehicle miles traveled—has increased 155 percent, and yet the EPA reports a dramatic decrease in every major pollutant it measures. Although driving is increasing by 1 to 3 percent each year, average vehicle emissions are dropping about 10 percent annually. Pollution will wane even more as motorists continue to replace older, dirtier cars with newer, cleaner models.

We're Paving Over America

How much of the United States is developed? Twenty-five percent? Fifty? Seventy-five? How about 5.4 percent? That's the Census Bureau's figure. And even much of that is not exactly crowded: The bureau says that an area is "developed" when it has 30 or more people per square mile.

But most people do live in developed areas, so it's easy to get the impression that humans have trampled nature. One need only take a cross-country flight and look down, however, to realize that our nation is mostly open space. And there are signs that Mother Nature is gaining ground. After furious tree chopping during America's early years, forests have made a comeback. The U.S. Forest Service notes that the "total area of forests has been fairly stable since about 1920." Agricultural innovations have a lot to do with this. Farmers can raise more on less land.

Yes, American houses are getting bigger. From 1970 to 2000, the average size ballooned from 1,500 square feet to 2,260. But this hardly means we're gobbling up ever more land. U.S. homeowners are using land more efficiently. Between 1970 and 2000, the average lot size shrank from 14,000 square feet to 10,000.

In truth, housing in this country takes up less space than most people realize. If the nation were divided into four-person households and each household had an acre, everyone would fit in an area half the size of Texas. The United States is not coming anywhere close to becoming an "Asphalt Nation," to use the title of a book by Jane Holtz Kay.

We Can't Deal with Global Warming Unless We Stop Driving

What should be done about global warming? The Kyoto Protocol seeks to get the world to agree to burn less fossil fuel and emit less carbon dioxide, and much of that involves driving less. But even disregarding the treaty's economic costs, Kyoto's environmental impact would be slight. Tom M.L. Wigley, chief scientist at the U.S. Center for Atmospheric Research, calculates that even if every nation met its obligation to reduce greenhouse gas, the Earth would be only .07 degrees centigrade cooler by 2050.

Wigley favors a much more stringent plan than Kyoto, but such restrictions would severely restrict economic growth, particularly in the developing world. Nations such as China and India were excluded from the Kyoto Protocol; yet if we're serious about reversing global warming by driving less, the developing world will have to be included.

The United Nations' Intergovernmental Panel on Climate Change [IPCC] notes that during the 20th century the Earth's temperature rose by 0.6 degrees centigrade and—depending on which of the many climate models turn out to be closest to reality—it expects the temperature to rise 1.4 to 5.8 degrees by 2100.

What does the IPCC think the effects of global warming may be? Flooding may increase. Infectious diseases may spread. Heat-related illness and death may increase. Yet as the IPCC notes repeatedly, the severity of such outcomes is enormously uncertain.

On the other hand, there's great certainty regarding who would be hurt the most: poor people in developing nations, especially those who lack clean, piped water and are thus vulnerable to waterborne disease. The IPCC points out that the quality of housing in those countries is important because simple measures such as adding screens to windows can help prevent diseases (including malaria, dengue and yellow fever) from entering homes. Fragile transportation systems can also frustrate disaster recovery efforts, as medical personnel are often unable to reach people trapped in flooded areas.

Dealing with global warming by building resilience against its possible effects is more productive . . . than trying to solve the problem by driving our automobiles less.

Two ways of dealing with global warming emerge. A more stringent version of Kyoto could be crafted to chase the unprecedented goal of trying to cool the atmosphere of the entire planet. Yet if such efforts resulted in lower economic growth, low-income populations in the United States and developing countries would be less able to protect themselves from the ill effects of extreme heat or other kinds of severe weather.

Alternatively, the focus could be on preventing the negative effects—the disease and death—that global warming might bring. Each year malaria kills 1 million to 3 million people, and one-third of the world's population is infected with water- or soil-borne parasitic diseases. It may well be that dealing with global warming by building resilience against its possible effects is more productive—and more realistic—than trying to solve the problem by driving our automobiles less.

There Is No Crisis over Disappearing Farmland or Open Space

Owen Courrèges

Owen Courrèges is a Research Fellow in the Urban Futures Program at the Reason Foundation, a public policy think tank promoting choice, competition, and a dynamic market economy.

A midst all the clamor for land use controls, there is one slogan that is hear[d] more often than any: "We need to protect America's farmland!" That is the battle cry of the 'open-space' protection movement, which evokes images of pastoral farmland being laid waste before the onslaught of urban sprawl, rendering America a never-ending expanse of strip malls and subdivisions. It's a chilling thought, and it would be a major problem to tackle—if it were real.

The Myth of Decreasing Farmland

Farmland, it turns out, is hardly an in-demand resource. Demand for farmland has decreased dramatically over the past several decades. More to the point, the so-called 'Green Revolution,' encompassing both high-yield crops and energy intensive agriculture, resulted in millions of acres of farmland being reclaimed by wilderness in the United States. The proliferation of biotechnology has expanded this trend and given it new life. In 1920, the US had some 600 million acres of wilderness. Today, estimates indicate that we have upwards of 140 million more.

Yet throughout this country, people are being led to believe that farmland ought to be preserved. In New Jersey, a new 'brownfields' initiative is aimed at creating more farmland

Owen Courrèges, "An Artificial Farmland Crisis," www.reason.org, July 7, 2004. Reproduced by permission.

in vacant lots for the purpose of sparing other farmland from development. In Gilroy, California, officials are asking property owners to join the 'Open Space Authority,' which would force them to pay $32 annually to fund farmland preservation efforts. The examples are endless. In every case, some class of people is expected to make a sacrifice for the sake of preserving a shrinking market—the market for farmland.

Open space isn't innately valuable. Aesthetic landscapes are nice for a Sunday drive, but little else.

Of course, no ill-advised policy is complete without federal involvement. As such, it should come as little surprise that the US Department of Agriculture (USDA) is on the forefront of open space preservation, justifying a seemingly absurd policy by appealing to the vague concept of "rural amenities." According to the USDA's website, "Local farmland losses continue to cause concern and motivate growing public support for farmland protection." However, there's little sign of a grassroots effort at work. For the most part, professional planners and advocacy groups are driving this movement, and the USDA has been sucked along for the ride.

Rural Amenities?

But what are these "rural amenities?" The USDA defines them as "open space, aesthetic landscapes, wildlife habitats, environmental services, agrarian cultural heritage, rural lifestyles, and recreational opportunities."

None of these makes much sense. Open space isn't innately valuable. Aesthetic landscapes are nice for a Sunday drive, but little else. Wildlife habitats aren't to be found in acres of corn—neither are environmental services. Agrarian cultural heritage and rural lifestyles won't rise or fall on land use controls. Oh, and you can't enjoy recreational opportunities on somebody else's farm. That's a good way to get shot at for trespassing.

That illustrates the problem with trying to derive a public benefit from private property. In the final analysis, the property is still privately owned and therefore the primary benefits are accrued by the owner. Farmers get to grow their crops. The best we get in return is a warm fuzzy from gazing at farmland. I can't speak for society at large, but from my perspective, that's a remarkably bad deal.

An Artificial Crisis

Moreover, there's an ideal solution waiting in the wings that nobody seems to have even considered: *just let the market handle it.*

Farmland won't disappear simply because the government doesn't act to protect it. There undoubtedly will be less of it in certain states with higher rates of urban development, but that merely reflects the reality that farmland isn't needed in those areas.

For instance, New Jersey isn't exactly an agrarian state. Their 'brownfields' program is an attempt to deny this, and to preserve remaining farmland in the state, but ultimately the inescapable fact is that society benefits more when land is used in the most efficient manner possible.

So what we have now is an artificial crisis. Farmland is indeed disappearing in many places, but it's actually a *good* thing. It's a good thing that areas where more urban development is needed are seeing more homes and commercial developments. It lowers housing costs and ensures economic growth. In this way, the market is the guarantor of a better future for everyone.

Yes, let the market handle the crisis over "open space." The only things we have to lose are our misconceptions.

Urban Sprawl in Some Cases Can Help Farmers

Wayne Wenzel

Wayne Wenzel is a writer for Farm Industry News, *a buying, product news, and technology magazine for high-income farmers in the Midwest.*

Farmers are supposed to hate urban sprawl. Encroaching subdivisions and Wal-Mart superstores take prime farmland out of production. The land, lifestyle and culture of an area are forever changed. But could it allow growers to trade in their farmland for several times as many acres somewhere else? If so, where? And what then?

As urban development encroaches, farmers are selling their prime farmland to developers at multiples of 6 to 15 times the value of agricultural land values. But most are not retiring as idle millionaires. Nor are most being pushed onto marginal acres. Rather, they are "trading out" their land for more acres of prime farmland further from the city. The growing phenomenon has been a major contributor to skyrocketing prices of prime farmland that can exceed $4,000/acre even for land far from any urban growth path.

Tax-Free Exchange

According to Dale Aupperle, president of Heartland Ag Group, Decatur, IL, more than 60% of farm real estate transactions in Macon County, IL, have been associated with a 1031 tax-free exchange of land acquired by residential and commercial developments. "Farming families understand agriculture and want to keep their money in agriculture," Aupperle says. "And they don't want to pay the tax, so the IRS 1031 exchange allows them to avoid the tax, or at least delay it."

Sometimes a farmer who sells at a development premium can multiply acreage by up to 10 times.

For farmers in the path of progress, a tax-free exchange means delaying the capital gains tax, in effect, getting interest-free money from the government to expand their business and multiply production. Taxes can be paid later, allowing the farmer to use that money to buy more property.

Sometimes a farmer who sells at a development premium can multiply acreage by up to 10 times. "Best of all," Aupperle says, "multiplying acres can also increase earnings 10-fold or more, depending on the area you are coming from."

Right now, Aupperle is noticing an increased volume of land for sale at the higher prices being bid by these exchange prices. "There is a 10% premium being paid by the exchange land buyer for prime farmland with significant size tracts. Farmers want prime tracts, they want large tracts, and they will pay a premium. It's shown in the marketplace," he says.

Are those values likely to hold? "Land prices are in an up trend, and I think we are very solid for the market we are trading in now, except for that premium being paid by exchange buyers who are the majority of the market," Aupperle says. "If the residential housing market slows, or the commercial boom slows, and the need for replacement property slows, that part of the demand could slow down and that 10% premium could disappear."

Bargains in Farmland

An old saying goes that cheap land is usually cheap for a reason. But as the price of prime farmland races ahead, is it still possible to find values and hidden gems? Aupperle thinks so. "Prime farmland is like a growth stock because it has two balanced components: annual earnings and appreciation in value," he explains. "It looks just like a growth stock of any major corporation on the stock exchange. Farmland is what it earns."

Following the land-as-stock analogy, a contrarian play could be to buy land that has been traditionally viewed as marginal in production. These are low-priced acres that, while perhaps not appreciating quickly or earning much income now, have the potential to do so in the future. What creates that potential? New technology.

"I believe there are excellent opportunities in the less productive areas because of better hybrids and varieties," Aupperle says. "In my market, that includes the southern third of Illinois and marginal areas of central and northern Illinois. Better hybrids and varieties with tolerance to stresses such as drought, insects, heat, and low-nutrient soils are going to allow the more marginal soils to produce with higher yields in good years. More importantly, they'll preserve yield in stressful years and minimize income fluctuations."

Better crop genetics are just part of the technology equation. Seed treatments or coatings allow planting in cooler soils. Variable-rate seed and fertilizer could make marginal soils more consistently productive. Soil moisture can be managed through tile drainage or irrigation. Improvements in these technologies, or new technologies still being developed, have the potential to turn marginal land into profitably productive land.

Urban Sprawl May Not Be So Bad for Wildlife

Space Daily

Space Daily is a daily news source for space industry professionals.

Urban sprawl might not be as harmful to wildlife as previously thought, according to a new study by researchers from the Landscape Analysis Lab at Sewanee: The University of the South in Tennessee.

Using field surveys and digital maps of habitat, David Haskell and Jonathan Evans, both biology professors at Sewanee and Neil Pelkey, an environmental science professor at Juniata College in Huntingdon, Pa., compared the diversity of bird populations in natural forests, tree plantations and "exurban" (urban sprawl) areas along the Cumberland Plateau in Tennessee.

[Sprawl] areas . . . have a mix of forest, ornamental shrubbery, lawns and other structures that provide diverse nesting opportunities for a wide variety of bird species.

Tree Plantations Versus Sprawl Areas

They found that tree plantations had substantially less bird population diversity than did native forests and exurban areas. In some cases, exurban areas had more diversity than did the native forests. "These findings suggest that urban sprawl is not all bad for wildlife," Haskell says. "This turns conventional wisdom about wildlife conservation on its head."

Space Daily, "Research Finds Urban Sprawl Not So Bad for Wildlife," www.spacedaily .com, January 13, 2007. Reproduced by permission.

For years scientists have been concerned with the loss of biodiversity resulting from worldwide deforestation. Governments and private organizations have implemented conservation programs that discourage sprawl and promote tree plantations to replace deforested areas. "Scientists had assumed that tree plantations were preferable to exurban areas for wildlife conservation," Haskell says. "This study firmly refutes this assumption, and has important implications for government policies, many of which subsidize plantations and penalize sprawl in the name of wildlife conservation."

For estimates of forest cover, the U.S. government classifies forest converted to tree plantation as "no loss of forest," and classifies wooded areas where houses have been built as "loss of forest." "Yet our data show that plantations have much lower levels of biodiversity than do native forests and that exurban areas can retain much of the biodiversity of native forests," the researchers write. "Therefore, current methods of accounting for forests give potentially misleading results for biodiversity analyses."

Haskell says that tree plantations have nearly doubled in acreage in the U.S. over the last 15 years to nearly 45 million acres, due in large part to government policies encouraging such land use.

The researchers believe that extensive chemical and mechanical land clearing techniques used to prepare land for tree plantation, along with the fact that most plantations contain only a single type of tree, result in poor nesting habitats for many types of birds. Exurban areas on the other hand have a mix of forest, ornamental shrubbery, lawns and other structures that provide diverse nesting opportunities for a wide variety of bird species.

CHAPTER 3

Does Urban Sprawl Contribute to the Decline of Cities?

Chapter Preface

Many anti-sprawl advocates observe that urban sprawl is essentially the flight of middle-class people and businesses from the inner cities, which leaves behind ever poorer urban residents. This abandonment of the inner cities, many commentators claim, has isolated and accelerated poverty within the urban center because reduced tax resources are unable to maintain schools, roads, and other publicly funded projects. Sprawl helps inner cities deteriorate. This process of urban decay tends to work along class and racial lines, as it adversely affects the poor and minorities the most. As businesses move out of the city, fewer jobs are available to those who remain behind, who rely on public transportation and have less education. Real estate becomes vacant, and in the face of desperation, crime may increase.

Ironically, some forms of urban renewal can also adversely affect poor populations. When downtown areas are rediscovered, when empty industrial sites are transformed into expensive lofts, and high-income people move into renewed urban centers—a trend called "gentrification"—adjacent housing may become more expensive in what were once low-income neighborhoods.

Many people point to Detroit, Michigan, as a prime example of this phenomenon. Once heralded as the Motor City, Detroit was the early twentieth century's world capital for automobile manufacturing and industrial wealth. However, according to the U.S. Census Bureau, the once-booming city lost 48.6 percent of its population between 1950 (pop. 1,849,568) and 2000 (pop. 951,270). This population drain coincided with a pattern of sprawl that saw substantial suburban growth. During these decades of population decline, urban Detroit had to maintain existing infrastructure with sharply reduced tax revenue. As a result, the quality of inner city schools suffered; road, water, and sewer maintenance declined; and city services such as police and fire were significantly downsized. The city became much more racially segregated, and poor, mostly African American residents struggled to survive amid the decay. The city's economy also contracted as businesses pulled out and young, educated workers migrated to the suburbs or to other cities or regions where job opportunities were better. The absence of quality education and good jobs contributed to a rise in violent crime and drug addiction, as people without hope began to prey on their neighbors.

Various efforts were made to redevelop Detroit's inner core, but the task proved daunting. In the early 2000s, amid considerable rebuilding, the city remained known mostly for its huge, sprawling suburbs and its downtown of vacant or abandoned real estate. The predominantly African American city is also one of the most racially segregated in the country. Meanwhile, Detroit's pro-automobile tradition fed resistance among suburban residents to any type of affordable or efficient public transportation. Revitalizing Detroit, many believed, would take not only enormous effort and funding, but also fundamental shifts in people's attitudes.

Other American cities have not experienced the same depopulation as Detroit but still have created urban sprawl. Los Angeles, California, for example, is one of the most sprawling urban areas in the country, but sharp population increases have kept both its downtown and outlying areas densely populated. In the case of Los Angeles and some other cities, urban sprawl may not be causing inner city decline.

This difference in urban growth patterns contributes to the controversy about urban sprawl. Although many commentators see the suburbs as a death knell for cities, others believe that urban sprawl in many places is a typical part of urban growth driven by the common inclination of people to live in single-family houses away from city congestion. In these days of natural coastal disasters, some experts even see the dispersal of populations and businesses away from a central core as healthier than traditional, high-density city formation. The contributors to this chapter present viewpoints that highlight both the positive and negative effects of urban sprawl on the nation's cities.

Urban Sprawl Has Impoverished U.S. Cities

Olga Bonfiglio

Olga Bonfiglio, a professor at Kalamazoo College, grew up in the Detroit area.

When leaders of the Archdiocese of Detroit began looking for solutions to the mounting poverty in the Detroit metropolitan area, they discovered that the traditional ministries of soup kitchens, clothing drives and holiday baskets were not changing the impoverished environment of the city. The city's decline was more structural, institutional and political, and they realized that they were looking squarely into an injustice that had developed and permeated the community for the past 40 years—urban sprawl. The archdiocese, which serves 1.5 million Catholics in six counties of southeastern Michigan, joined a coalition of interfaith religious congregations that is working hard not only to curb and contain urban sprawl, but also to approach it as a moral issue that demands a response of justice and equality for all people living in the region.

Effects of Sprawl

Urban sprawl is a consequence of federal, state and local land-use policies that have resulted in an epidemic of unplanned growth, the voracious consumption of land and gross inequality among people in a region. Sprawl is deemed responsible for abandoned buildings, run-down neighborhoods, poor schools, pot-holed roads, polluted lakes and streams and feelings of alienation and disconnection among residents and their communities.

"We have caused the problem. It seems logical that we can deal with it," said Dan Piepszowski, director of Christian Service for the archdiocese, the division heading up the fight against sprawl. "We have to be uncomfortable with communities that are isolated racially or economically or socially. That's not a good healthy thing for the church," he added.

In 1990, 67 percent of new growth occurred in the metropolitan areas. Now [2002] 80 percent of new growth occurs in suburbs.

"Detroit was the envy of New York and Chicago 40 or 50 years ago," said Ann Serra, director of grants and metropolitan equity for the archdiocese, another leader in the effort. "There was a lot of money here because of manufacturing. No one would have thought Detroit could become what it is now. We were at the top."

The Role of Transportation

According to Ms. Serra, Detroit began its downward economic spiral in the 1950's when manufacturing began to move to the South as a means of avoiding high labor costs. The riot of 1967 accelerated the depopulation of the city. In the early 1970's bussing mandates to desegregate schools encouraged more movement of white Detroiters outward to a ring of suburbs around the city. Freeway construction accompanied that movement, and millions of dollars were spent in building that accommodated an increase in automobile transportation and weakened the public transportation system's route scheduling and accessibility. "There were restrictions on bus routes along racial lines," said Ms. Serra. White people did not want to ride a bus with black people, and buses did not go out to the suburbs where the jobs were. Black people who lived in the city could not get a ride to their jobs. Indeed, one of the key issues surrounding sprawl is transportation. So the archdiocese is also working to promote a mass transit system in the south-eastern Michigan region.

"The nation's transportation system is a kind of apartheid," said Dr. Robert Bullard, a sociologist from Clark Atlanta University in Atlanta, Ga., and a leading national expert on race and the environment. Mr. Bullard spoke last fall [2001] at the Conference on Living in Justice and Solidarity sponsored by the archdiocese. "It was set up to create racial, economic, social and geographical barriers in our communities."

Sprawl encourages local communities to adopt self-defeating behavior patterns that negatively affect economic development.

"We are a suburban nation," said Mr. Bullard, citing that in 1990, 67 percent of new growth occurred in the metropolitan areas. Now [2002] 80 percent of new growth occurs in suburbs, where mostly white people live. In Detroit, 70 percent of the office space is located outside the city and out of reach of the many central city dwellers who need jobs and the transportation necessary to get to those jobs. One-third of the people do not own cars and most are poor and non-white. They rely on public transportation to get them to work, stores and social activities. But because of Detroit's limited public transportation system, only 2 percent of the population uses the system—as compared to cities like New York where 47 percent of the population get around on buses and trains.

The Detroit Example

The archdiocese has been educating Catholics about sprawl and its effects on the region since 1999. It hired Myron Orfield, president of the Metropolitan Area Research Corporation in Minneapolis and author of a groundbreaking book, *Metropolitics: Social Separation and Sprawl*, as a consultant on this project. He spoke at the fall conference, too. "As population decreases, property values decrease, business disinvests in that community, and poorer people move in," said Mr. Orfield. But he said that the decline of Detroit goes much deeper. It turns out that the first ring of suburbs is declining and a second ring has been developing during the 1990's. According to Mr. Orfield, the Detroit metropolitan area has increased in land area by 30 percent, while the city's population—which peaked in 1950 at two million—is now half that size.

Mr. Orfield cites the example of Macomb County, north of Detroit, where the centrally located older suburban bedroom communities of Warren, Centerline, East Pointe and Fraser are losing middle-class residents to newer developments out on the edges of the county. Because these communities do not have much of an industrial or commercial tax base, they provide fewer resources and services per household and are experiencing physical deterioration. Poorer people are either left there or they are moving in. "Part of the problem in Detroit is the historical pattern equating prosperity with movement away from the city to the suburbs," said Mr. Piepszowski. People left the city feeling pushed out because of crime, bad schools and drugs. They also feel pulled out because of government policies and incentives that favor growth.

Today white people still blame black people for the decline of the city, while black people see sprawl as white people's problem.

Sprawl encourages local communities to adopt self-defeating behavior patterns that negatively affect economic development in their own backyards as well as those of their neighbors. Mr. Piepszowski noted that southeastern Michigan local governments compete with one another instead of cooperating for business development. This "creates an impediment to economic growth and prosperity for the whole region," he observed. Any talk about regional government and planning makes people suspicious that they might be asked to bail out Detroit, so they resist any attempts in that direction. Mr. Piepszowski said that resistance to regional approaches comes from the same pride and healthy parochialism that built these communities. But such an attitude also reduces the region's ability to attract businesses looking for an area that provides a support system of education, housing, a diverse labor pool and adequate transportation networks.

A Racial Divide

In fact, the history of regional approaches in Detroit has not been encouraging, including approaches advocated by the archdiocese. In the 1970's, for example, the archdiocese's support of bussing for the purpose of providing all races with equal opportunities for education helped to spark white flight to the suburbs. Today white people still blame black people for the decline of the city, while black people see sprawl as white people's problem. Mr. Piepszowski said that unless all the citizens of the region attack sprawl together, a backlash against regionalism might create more segregation.

"What drives Detroit is race," said the Rev. Steve Jones, pastor of First Baptist Church in Birmingham. Reverend Jones is part of a growing of interfaith coalition pastors that is working with the archdiocese to curb sprawl. Birmingham is one of the older suburbs of Detroit and home to high-income executives of the automobile companies. "You just can't get away from [race]" said the Rev. Jones. "It permeates everything we're about. Detroit is the most segregated metropolitan area [in the country]. It just passed Gary, Ind." He contends that race is one of the reasons why Detroiters have traditionally avoided building a mass transit system, too. "We can't imagine sitting on a bus with people different from us," he said. "We don't trust one another and we don't trust the differences. What's more, we don't have any practice [dealing with people who are different from ourselves]."

Learning to Live Together

Cognizant of the racial divisions in the region, Mr. Piepszowski argues that people must learn more about others' faiths and lifestyles and learn to live with one another. "We Catholics have to be comfortable with diversity both internationally and domestically." Mr. Piepszowski points to Southfield as a gem of community diversity. An older, formerly white suburb in northwest Detroit, it now contains Armenians, African Americans, Chaldeans, Jews and Russians living together. Such cities, he said, provide wonderful models of racial and cultural mixes.

The archdiocese's Christian Service Department relies on parishioners to assume the leadership for this new anti-sprawl ministry. It sees the ministry as another opportunity to build lay leadership. And laypeople are readily assuming their roles as leaders.

"We are getting a much better response from people as they become part of a public discourse," said Ann Serra, who remembers the hopelessness she witnessed during the first meetings of the new anti-sprawl ministry. In the suburban parishes she heard horrible stories about Coleman Young (the former black mayor of Detroit) and his policies, as well as people's fears about the migration and decline in the area. Now Ms. Serra conducts a dialogue with participants. She begins by first asking them why they chose the community they live in. Invariably they say, because of the schools, safety and lower taxes. No one has listed accessibility to shopping or highways. "What we are trying to do [through the sprawl issue] is build solidarity in the church," she said. "Everyone is learning as we dialogue. The people see that we're all Catholics, regardless of race, and that we have obligations to one another, whether we live in the city or the suburbs."

The archdiocese has been contacting all its 314 parishes to join in this ministry against sprawl and to promote a regional mass transit system in southeastern Michigan. It has also teamed up with a local community organizing group called

Moses (Metropolitan Organizing Strategy Enabling Strength), which works with other religious congregations in the city and suburbs on this issue. Moses provides a training program that teaches citizens how to take responsibility and mobilize for change in a democratic way. Residents learn how to build citizen coalitions from a position of power and action. "To be powerful is a good thing," said Bill O'Brien, executive director of Moses. "To be powerless is a scandal. Power is the ability to act. Through power we teach church leaders how to organize people and/or money." O'Brien said that people become empowered because they are in relationship with individuals and groups of people. "The church is a place of relationship and community. We provide people with a strategy to make that happen."

Pushing for Mass Transit

Archdiocesan leaders and other church organizers [saw] the elections of 2002 as an opportunity to assert their power for a regional mass transit system. The state [underwent] a huge turnover in leadership. Because of the state's term-limits law, there [was] a change of governor as well as of 30 percent of its representatives and 70 percent of its state senators. Kwame Kilpatrick became Detroit's new mayor . . . [in 2002] after coming from the Michigan state legislature, where he sponsored a regional transportation bill.

Connections between the city and suburbs through . . . [the] battle against sprawl . . . are key to the . . . hopes for promoting justice.

"But the transportation network is just rubber and steel unless the relational pieces come into play," cautioned Mr. Piepszowski, who recognizes that there are still some political hold-outs against a mass transit system. "Transportation is a social delivery system. It's about people. Solving our transportation problems in the Detroit metropolitan area is one way to overcome inequality among people here. As Catholics, we come to our faith as a community. Catholic teaching is all about building community."

Ann Serra remains optimistic, too. "When you are connected, you see others' problems," she said. And relationships among church people, connections between the city and suburbs through this battle against sprawl—and for mass transit—are key to the archdiocese's hopes for promoting justice in the Detroit metropolitan area.

Bigger, Older Cities Continue to Lose Populations

Associated Press

The Associated Press *is a news organization that serves as a source of new, photos, graphics, audio and video for thousands of daily newspaper, radio, television, and online customers around the world.*

Elk Grove, California, wasn't even incorporated six years ago, and now it's the fastest-growing city in America. Bigger, older cities are losing ground. The Sacramento suburb grew by 11.6 percent last year, to 112,000 people, typifying America's appetite for open spaces, affordable homes and suburban living. Once a rural farming community, Elk Grove has given way to sprawling development, fueled by a short commute to Sacramento and local employers such as Apple Computer. "Ten to 15 years ago is when the housing started coming in. That was followed by the businesses," says Janet Toppenberg, president and CEO of the Elk Grove Chamber of Commerce.

Migration Patterns

Americans have been moving west and south for decades, and last year [2005] was no different. All but three of the 50 fastest-growing cities from 2004 to 2005 were in those regions of the country, with many in California and Florida, according to Census Bureau estimates Wednesday. The estimates were for cities with populations of 100,000 or more. Elk Grove was followed in the top five by North Las Vegas, Nevada; Port St. Lucie, Florida; Gilbert, Arizona, and Cape Coral, Florida. All five are suburban, and all have fewer than 200,000 residents. "We have a pattern that is consistent across the country," said Hans

Johnson, a research fellow at the Public Policy Institute of California. "Families choose to move to areas where they can buy more housing for less money and often with better schools."

Americans also are moving away from many of the nation's biggest cities, though the reasons vary with the cities. People are following jobs out of struggling Midwestern cities. Others are leaving expensive Northeastern and Western cities in search of more affordable homes. And people are fleeing big cities everywhere in search of better schools.

Most of the big cities that gained population were in the South.

New York remained America's largest city, with 8.1 million people. The city has added 135,000 people since 2000, but it lost 21,500 from 2004 to 2005, more than any other city. Detroit, with its struggling economy, has lost 65,000 people since 2000, the most of any city. Philadelphia, which has lost about 50,000 manufacturing jobs since 2000, has lost 54,000 people during the same period. San Francisco, with the highest real estate prices in the United States, has lost 37,000 people since 2000, according to the Census Bureau. The bureau issues annual population estimates based on building permits, housing units and other changes since its 2000 headcount.

Some Exceptions

States sometimes dispute those estimates based on their own calculations. For example, California officials estimate that San Francisco has grown by 22,000 people since 2000, rather than shrinking. But even if the city did add people, it did so at a much slower rate than cities in the center of the state, said John Malson, a research manager for the state Department of Finance. "The housing market out here has gone nuts, especially in the coastal areas," Malson said. "The Central Valley is still more affordable than the coast," he added. "A lot of people are moving out from the (San Francisco) Bay area."

Most of the big cities that gained population were in the South, according to the Census Bureau. In overall numbers, Phoenix added the most people—44,400—from 2004 to 2005, giving it a population of nearly 1.5 million.

New Orleans, an exception in the South, had already lost population before Hurricane Katrina. The city lost about 30,000 people from 2000 to 2005, setting its population at 455,000, the Census Bureau said in an estimate made before the hurricane scattered hundreds of thousands of people. Local officials estimate that New Orleans has rebounded to about 221,000 people since the storm.

Inner Cities Continue to Decline Economically

Daniel Muniz

Daniel Muniz is the editor of National Summary, *a Web site that publishes in-depth analyses and commentary on current events and social issues.*

For those who loathe and decry urban sprawl, the news has been dismal but hardly a surprise. According to a Harvard University study based from 1995 to 2003, about half of the count's 82 largest municipalities lost jobs. And in sharp contrast during the same period, just one surrounding suburban metropolitan area lost any jobs.

Also, investment by businesses does not happen deep inside of a city even when the federal government throws billions of dollars at it as confirmed by a separate analysis by the *Associated Press* [AP]. AP discovered that none of the best-performing cities even participated in the federal empowerment zone and renewal community programs. They simply performed better without government assistance. And this assistance was supposed to provide tax incentives so that businesses in certain depressed areas of a city could expand by hiring new employees. It never happened.

Overregulation and Hostility

But what went wrong? Why don't businesses want to relocate to the inner city or at least bring in a little bit more commercial development? Brian Sullivan, a spokesman for the Department of Housing and Urban Development, said: *"We're not trying to preach to people that you are over-regulating . . . but it is true that in some parts of the country the regulatory climate puts out the unwelcome mat."*

Daniel Muniz, "Urban Sprawl Rules: Inner Cities Continue Decline," *National Summary*, July 24, 2007. www.nationalsummary.com. Reproduced by permission.

Excessive red tape is part of the equation but hostility in general is what created the problem in the first place. In my hometown of San Antonio, Texas, I have seen numerous community leaders of depressed parts of the city clamor about needing more commercial development in their neighborhoods. In all reality, strong economic activity is what will transform blighted neighborhoods. Sadly, when big corporations do try to either invest or expand, they are often met with fierce and often virulent opposition, many times by the same community leaders who wanted them there in the first place.

For instance, a large regional supermarket chain had a location deep inside the inner city. The chain wanted to expand its present store and bought up some of the surrounding land. During this process, community activists combed all the nearby neighborhoods for people to sign petitions to stop the development. Some of the activists' arguments did have merit such as how the roads could accommodate increased traffic, etc.

But most of the complaints were downright ludicrous such as demanding input in employee benefits, management practices, and involvement in other financial aspects of the company. In addition, the activists brought out inflammatory and incendiary accusations from global warming to exploitation of Third-World workers, and about every other left-wing cause. About the only thing they didn't do was accuse management of stealing children.

Sadly, the free market is exactly what will help . . . depressed areas of town.

Naturally, the supermarket chain rejected almost all of the activist demands and then pointed to its involvement in community activities as a responsible corporate citizen and its numerous donations to local charities. They also explained the economic benefit that they would bring to the neighborhood as well as being part of the catalyst that could bring more development to the area. The activists were not swayed.

In fact, it is just about impossible to persuade such community leaders since they have a deep suspicion of the free market and the free economy itself. Sadly, the free market is exactly what will help such depressed areas of town. The more financial investments that are made will attract more economic development.

But the activists don't see it that way. They encourage city governments to impose more restrictions and more regulations. And unless it is on their terms, most activist groups will oppose just about any kind of economic development. Unfortunately, it is nearly impossible for companies to make any sort of profits by acquiescing to their demands.

Businesses Welcomed in Suburbs

In contrast, the suburbs are different. They actually want the big retail strip centers, the shopping malls, and big office buildings. They want development and they don't mind coexisting with it. Not surprisingly, economic development goes to where it is welcomed, encouraged, and even nurtured.

I remember near the time I graduated high school; the same regional supermarket chain had a location far out into the suburbs which was close to where I lived. The chain acquired a much larger vacant lot nearby to build a bigger store. The response was tremendous. The suburbanites packed the larger store and were delighted to have a better selection of products at a place nearby. The opposition to this development was practically nonexistent.

And that has pretty much been the story of the suburbs of my teens. My parents still live there and I am often amazed at how much investment that the area has attracted. Huge retail shops, movie theaters, and plenty of other business activity in places that were just empty ranch land during my teenage years. My parents really don't have to drive very far at all which was a different story when I was in high school.

But the story is not much different in other suburbs. What was once desolate is now brimming with shops and economic activity. And on a larger scale, this process has repeated itself across the country.

Bringing Development Back to Cities

So what can be done to bring development back inside the city? First, end the hypocrisy. Community leaders cannot have it both ways. Complain about the lack of business activity and then become hostile to the companies that do want to invest. And that leads up to the next step.

End the hostility. Many depressed areas of a city represent a huge market to businesses. Developers want to go to the inner city and hawk their products and services to an underserved segment of the population. Unfortunately, activist groups and local government officials fight them every step of the way even though their investments benefits that part of town.

But the inverse to ending hostility is to embrace the free market. And that is the major sticking point that usually ends all discussion. So until community leaders realize that big corporate investment in their area will bring about prosperity instead of oppression, their neighborhoods will continue to be depressed and forsaken.

Urban Sprawl Is an Inherent Part of Urbanization

Witold Rybczynski

Witold Rybczynski is the architecture critic for Slate, *an online magazine.*

We hate sprawl. It's responsible for everything that we don't like about modern American life: strip malls, Mc-Mansions, big-box stores, the loss of favorite countryside, the decline of downtowns, traffic congestion, SUVs, high gas consumption, dependence on foreign oil, the Iraq war. No doubt about it, sprawl is bad, American bad. Like expanding waistlines, it's touted around the world as yet another symptom of our profligacy and wastefulness as a nation. Or, as Robert Bruegmann puts it in his new book, "cities that sprawl and, by implication, the citizens living in them, are self indulgent and undisciplined."

A Historical Phenomenon

Or not. In *Sprawl*, cheekily subtitled *A Compact History*, Bruegmann, a professor of art history at the University of Illinois at Chicago, examines the assumptions that underpin most people's strongly held convictions about sprawl. His conclusions are unexpected. To begin with, he finds that urban sprawl is not a recent phenomenon: It has been a feature of city life since the earliest times. The urban rich have always sought the pleasures of living in low-density residential neighborhoods on the outskirts of cities. As long ago as the Ming dynasty in the 14th century, the Chinese gentry sang the praises of the exurban life, and the rustic *villa suburbana* was a common feature of ancient Rome. Pliny's maritime villa was 17 miles from the city, and many fashionable Roman villa districts such as Tusculum—where Cicero had a summer house—were much closer. Bruegmann also observes that medieval suburbs—those urbanized areas outside cities' protective walls—had a variety of uses. Manufacturing processes that were too dirty to be located inside the city (such as brick kilns, tanneries, slaughterhouses) were in the suburbs; so were the homes of those who could not afford to reside within the city proper. This pattern continued during the Renaissance. Those compact little cities bounded by bucolic landscapes, portrayed in innumerable idealized paintings, were surrounded by extensive suburbs.

According to the *Oxford English Dictionary*, "sprawl" first appeared in print in this context in 1955, in an article in the London *Times* that contained a disapproving reference to "great sprawl" at the city's periphery. But, as Bruegmann shows, by then London had been spreading into the surrounding countryside for hundreds of years. During the 17th and 18th centuries, while the poor moved increasingly eastward, affluent Londoners built suburban estates in the westerly direction of Westminster and Whitehall, commuting to town by carriage. These areas are today the Central West End; one generation's suburb is the next generation's urban neighborhood. As Bruegmann notes, "Clearly, from the beginning of modern urban history, and contrary to much accepted wisdom, suburban development was very diverse and catered to all kinds of people and activities." When inexpensive public transportation opened up South London for development in the 19th century, London sprawl took a different form: streets and streets of small brick-terrace houses. For middle-class families, this dispersal was a godsend, since it allowed them to exchange a cramped flat for a house with a garden. The outward movement continued in the boom years between the First and Second World Wars, causing the built-up area of

London to double, although the population increased by only about 10 percent—which sounds a lot like Atlanta today.

> *While the common perception is that sprawl is America's contribution to urban culture, . . . it appeared in Europe first.*

It was not only by sprawling at the edges that cities reduced their densities. Preindustrial cities began life by exhibiting what planners call a steep "density gradient," that is, the population density was extremely high in the center and dropped off rapidly at the edges. Over time, with growing prosperity—and the availability of increasingly far-reaching mass transportation (omnibuses, streetcars, trains, subways, cars)—this gradient flattened out. Density at the center reduced while density in the (expanding) suburbs increased. The single most important variable in this common pattern was, as Bruegmann observes, not geography or culture, but the point at which the city reached economic maturity. In the case of London, the city's population density peaked in the early 19th century; in Paris it happened in the 1850s; and in New York City in the early 1900s. While the common perception is that sprawl is America's contribution to urban culture, Bruegmann shows that it appeared in Europe first.

Yet haven't high rates of automobile ownership, easy availability of land, and a lack of central planning made sprawl much worse in the United States? Most American tourists spend their time visiting historic city centers, so they may be unaware that suburbs now constitute the bulk of European metropolitan areas, just as they do in America. We marvel at the efficiency of European mass transit, but since 1950, transit ridership has remained flat, while the use of private automobiles has skyrocketed. Just as in America. "As cities across Europe have become more affluent in the last decades of the twentieth century," Bruegmann writes, "they have witnessed a continuing decline in population densities in the historic core, a quickening of the pace of suburban and exurban development, a sharp rise in automobile ownership and use, and the proliferation of subdivisions of single-family houses and suburban shopping centers." Despite some of the most stringent anti-sprawl regulations in the world and high gas prices, the population of the city of Paris has declined by almost a third since 1921, while its suburbs have grown. Over the last 15 years, the city of Milan has lost about 600,000 people to its metropolitan fringes, while Barcelona, considered by many a model compact city, has developed extensive suburbs and has experienced the largest population loss of any European city in the last 25 years. Greater London, too, continues to sprawl, resulting in a population density of 12,000 persons per square mile, about half that of New York City.

Sprawl is and always has been inherent to urbanization.

Reasons for Sprawl

The point is not that London, any more than Barcelona or Paris, is a city in decline (although the demographics of European city centers have changed and are now home to wealthier and older inhabitants, just like some American cities). Central urban densities are dropping because household sizes are smaller and affluent people occupy more space. Like Americans, Europeans have opted for decentralization. To a great extent, this dispersal is driven by a desire for home-ownership. "Polls consistently confirm that most Europeans, like most Americans, and indeed most people worldwide, would prefer to live in single-family houses on their own piece of land rather than in apartment buildings," Bruegmann writes. So strong is this preference that certain European countries such as Ireland and the United Kingdom now have higher single-family house occupancy rates than the United States, while others, such as Holland, Belgium, and Norway, are comparable. Half of all French households now live in houses.

It appears that *all* cities—at least all cities in the industrialized Western world—have experienced a dispersal of population from the center to a lower-density periphery. In other words, sprawl is universal. Why is this significant? "Most American anti-sprawl reformers today believe that sprawl is a recent and peculiarly American phenomenon caused by specific technological innovations like the automobile and by government policies like single-use zoning or the mortgage-interest deduction on the federal income tax," Bruegmann writes. "It is important for them to believe this because if sprawl turned out to be a long-standing feature of urban development worldwide, it would suggest that stopping it involves something much more fundamental than correcting some poor American land-use policy."

What this iconoclastic little book demonstrates is that sprawl is not the anomalous result of American zoning laws, or mortgage interest tax deduction, or cheap gas, or subsidized highway construction, or cultural antipathy toward cities. Nor is it an aberration. Bruegmann shows that asking whether sprawl is "good" or "bad" is the wrong question. Sprawl is and always has been inherent to urbanization. It is driven less by the regulations of legislators, the actions of developers, and the theories of city planners, than by the decisions of millions of individuals—Adam Smith's "invisible hand." This makes altering it very complicated, indeed. There are scores of books offering "solutions" to sprawl. Their authors would do well to read this book. To find solutions—or, rather, better ways to manage sprawl, which is not the same thing—it helps to get the problem right.

Urban Sprawl Has Kept Housing Prices Affordable in Cities that Have Not Tried to Restrict Suburban Growth

Wendell Cox

Wendell Cox is a senior fellow of The Heartland Institute, a nonprofit organization in Chicago, Illinois, that promotes free-market solutions to social and economic problems. Cox is also a consultant to public-policy, planning, and transportation organizations; and a visiting professor at a French national university.

For various reasons, Montreal [Canada] has been losing economic ground to Toronto and other North American urban areas over the last decades. But this could be changing. Politics and infrastructure are combining to substantially improve the competitiveness of the Montreal region.

An Absence of Regulation

In the Montreal area, as in all other urban areas in western Europe and North America, nearly all employment and population growth has occurred in the suburbs in recent decades and the automobile has become the dominant mode of transportation. Suburbanization (pejoratively called "urban sprawl") has made it possible for unprecedented numbers of households to own their own homes and accumulate capital that otherwise would have simply enriched their landlords.

The automobile has greatly improved mobility and the ability of people to take jobs throughout urban areas. As a result, it has been a major factor in driving the post-Second World War economic growth that has created a widespread, "democratized" prosperity.

Wendell Cox, "The Upside of Sprawl: Suburbs and Roads Lower Housing Costs and Boost Development," *The Gazette*, June 21, 2006. Reproduced by permission.

What sets Montreal apart is that these two generators of better lives, suburbanization and the automobile, have not so far been the target of serious government restrictions.

In Canada and in other high-income nations, some urban areas have adopted policies to limit suburbanization. They have, like Portland, Ore., Sydney, Australia, and Vancouver, B.C., adopted urban growth boundaries that seek to force all growth within a prescribed area. The effort to stop urban expansion has created a scarcity of land for new homes and businesses. This has raised the price of land substantially and in consequence, the price of housing. Today, housing prices relative to incomes in Vancouver are approaching double that of Montreal. Portland's urban-growth boundary was a factor in driving housing prices relative to incomes up at a faster rate than in any other major U.S. metropolitan area during the 1990s.

Montreal's principal competitor, Toronto, is the most recent convert to affordability-destroying anti-suburban policies, with the Ontario government's decision to create a greenbelt where development will be prohibited. The Montreal area, however, has resisted these overly restrictive land use policies. As a result, here, as in Winnipeg, fast-growing Edmonton, Atlanta, Dallas-Fort Worth and Houston, housing prices remain at historical norms relative to incomes.

Late information from the U.S. Census Bureau indicates the most unaffordable housing markets (all of which have anti-suburban policies) are now experiencing significant out-migration of residents.

The Need for Roads

Many of the same urban areas have adopted anti-automobile strategies, seeking to attract people to transit. There is no disputing transit's superiority for commuting to large, concentrated downtown areas, such as in Montreal. But downtowns contain, on average, one-fifth or less of urban employment.

No urban area in western Europe or North America provides the automobile-competitive transit that would be capable of providing mobility to the other four-fifths of jobs.

There is an increasing recognition of the importance of highways to economic growth.

This means that high-capacity roadways are necessary. This is much more than a matter of minimizing travel time to work. More freely flowing highways mean that trucking costs are less and that service vehicles can reach their destinations quicker. All of this brings lower prices and more discretionary income.

There is an increasing recognition of the importance of highways to economic growth. Studies in Vancouver and Portland have made a strong case for improving traffic congestion by additional highway investment. In Portland, a driving force has been the fact businesses are beginning to locate in other urban areas because of the increase in traffic congestion that has resulted from neglecting necessary highway expansions. The choice is not between transit and roads. The choice is rather between more and less traffic congestion. The choice is also between more and less economic growth.

Montreal already has one of the world's best expressway systems. Nonetheless, significant improvements are required. Perhaps the most important is the need to provide an alternative to the Metropolitan Boulevard and more river-crossing capacity.

While other urban areas pursue policies that restrict mobility and raise housing prices, Montreal's competitive position is likely to improve.

Quebec has adopted a program that will result in significant mobility improvements, including an expressway bypass of Montreal Island through the South Shore with a river-crossing upstream from Montreal Island. Building a new bridge to the South Shore, as recommended by the recent Nicolet Commission, would also greatly help improve mobility and reduce congestion. Additional transit investments should be undertaken only where they reduce hours of travel delay at a lower government cost than other alternatives.

Montreal and provincial officials should not succumb to the pessimistic and alarmist reports calling for a crackdown on car use and regulations to prevent suburban development. While other urban areas pursue policies that restrict mobility and raise housing prices, Montreal's competitive position is likely to improve and the region faces a brighter future.

CHAPTER 4

Should Urban Sprawl Be Restricted?

Chapter Preface

The main strategy for containing urban sprawl focuses on limiting and/or directing urban growth and development in various ways. Often called Smart Growth in the United States, this strategy attempts to concentrate growth in city centers or in urban pockets designated for development in order to preserve existing, sparsely populated farmland and surrounding open spaces. The goal is to encourage compact urban development that allows people to walk, bicycle, or use public transportation for shopping and commuting to jobs and schools. To accomplish this goal, Smart Growth employs a number of tactics, some of which involve redevelopment policies and zoning to create mixed-use communities (i.e., housing combined with businesses, entertainment, and other uses). Smart Growth policies also usually emphasize locating development near public transportation in order to discourage automobile use. Often, too, parks are considered a necessary part of new developments, in order to provide communities with access to recreational outdoor spaces.

Smart Growth advocates also urge the establishment of urban growth boundaries (UGBs)—essentially regional boundaries that separate urban land from rural land. Typically, areas inside the UGB are designated for higher density urban development and areas outside the UGB are limited in their growth by being designated for low density rural development. Local governments then use these boundaries as a guide when making zoning or other land use and development decisions.

Oregon, Washington, and Tennessee have mandated statewide use of UGBs, and more than 100 individual cities and counties across the United States have adopted them as well. Notable examples of UGBs are seen in Portland, Oregon; San Francisco, California; and Minneapolis, Minnesota. Outside the United States, growth-limiting boundaries have been adopted in the Canadian cities of Vancouver, British Columbia, and Toronto, Ontario, and in countries such as Great Britain and Australia.

UGBs have become increasingly controversial, however, because of their effects on the real estate market. Critics claim that establishing artificial boundaries for development limits the supply of usable land and drives up land and home prices. The effects of high housing prices, critics say, are felt mainly by low- and middle-income consumers who need to live near their urban jobs. In Portland, Oregon, for example, after the adoption of UGB policies, average housing density increased dramatically while housing prices soared. The city now ranks among the 10 percent least affordable housing markets in the nation. A similar pattern emerged in Napa County, California, where home prices, both within and outside the UGB boundaries, increased dramatically. Consumers in UGB areas tend to buy bigger houses on smaller lots, trading yards, and open space for interior square footage. Some wealthier consumers, however, can still afford to buy large lots in rural areas for custom homes. Problems have also arisen with plans to fund public transportation systems as part of UGB and Smart Growth policies.

Supporters of UGBs dismiss these criticisms, pointing out that housing prices have risen across the country, including areas that do not have growth boundaries in place. Also, Smart Growth advocates say Portland's housing prices are still less than in other parts of the West, an area that attracts growing numbers of people. Indeed, various studies have concluded that UGBs are not a major factor in higher housing costs in areas such as Portland. These studies show that home prices are based on a number of factors, such as home design, construction costs, financing, and raw land. And raw land costs—which is the factor influenced by UGBs—make up only about one-seventh of the price of new homes in Portland. The main factor influencing rising housing prices, many studies conclude, is not UGB restrictions, but rather a region's growth in employment and population—that is, the amount of increased demand for housing.

Whether good or bad, UGB policies remain one of several strategies being used by land-use professionals to limit urban sprawl. The only other serious proposals for protecting wild and rural spaces tend to involve population controls—usually an even more unpopular idea. Various pros and cons of these Smart Growth and population-based solutions to sprawl are discussed in the viewpoints in this chapter.

Smart Growth Developments Are Effective and Becoming Commonplace in American Cities

Mark Alden Branch

Mark Alden Branch is executive editor of the Yale Alumni Magazine *and writes frequently about architecture and design.*

While urban sprawl in America is far from being tamed, it is heartening to realize that not long ago, mixed-use, higher-density, and pedestrian-friendly developments were seen as novelties at best, and pie-in-the-sky dream worlds at worst. But now, several factors—the evangelism of New Urbanism promoters, the increased appeal of urban living, and the dire need for relief from the effects of sprawl—have made such development normative, if not yet dominant.

Particularly in the western United States, new mass-transit systems are providing the impetus for high-density, mixed-use development at or near transit stations. In Dallas alone, $800 million in development occurred along that city's new light-rail system between 1996 and 2001. Denver, Seattle, Portland, Oregon, and several cities in California are all actively promoting transit-oriented development and increased density along public transportation lines.

All well and good, says architect and planner Stefanos Polyzoides, but just how urban are some of these developments? "I'm discouraged by the suburban developers who come into cities and put in density without any serious interest in urban character," he says. A cofounder of the Congress for New Urbanism (CNU), Polyzoides is adamant that just increasing

Mark Alden Branch, "Smart Growth? Antisprawl Developments Are Getting Mixed Reviews," *Architecture*, vol. 92, iss. 7, July 2003, pp. 27–28. Copyright © 2003 Mark Alden Branch. Reproduced by permission.

density and mixing uses is not enough: Design—and architectural style—are critical, he says.

Fitting In

Polyzoides points to two projects by his own Pasadena, California-based firm, Moule & Polyzoides, that are currently in development along the Gold Line light-rail corridor that runs from Los Angeles to Pasadena. Mission Station in South Pasadena is a 1.65-acre, half-block development with 67 condominiums and 5,000 square feet of retail space. It lies adjacent to a transit station and between a community center and a neighborhood of bungalows. The residential units, which resemble single-family houses, attempt to fit into the local context, though at a higher density than their neighbors.

Del Mar Station, on the edge of downtown Pasadena, surrounds a Gold Line station with 347 housing units, 20,000 square feet of retail, and an underground parking garage for 1,200 cars. Here, the station is the centerpiece of a denser urban project. A public plaza with a campanile and retail shops sits at the station stop and acts as a "gateway to the city," the architects say. On one side of this space are multistory apartment buildings with retail space at plaza level; on the other side, between the plaza and a public park, are smaller-scale Mediterranean-style retail buildings.

Advocates of transit-oriented development . . . are still frustrated that the idea hasn't taken off more quickly.

"The point is that not all transit stops are the same, and there is no one-size-fits-all solution," says Polyzoides. "The goal is to see what is there and what could be there. Transit-oriented development is nothing more than appropriate urban development. It can be at a variety of scales."

Although projects like those in Pasadena are easier to realize than before, advocates of transit-oriented development (TOD)—that is, new development near bus or rail stations that is designed to be pedestrian-friendly and reduce car trips—are still frustrated that the idea hasn't taken off more quickly. Such development has been part of the discourse in architectural and planning circles for more than 15 years, but finding a way to make TODs happen has been difficult, according to Hank Dittmar, president of the advocacy group Reconnecting America and chair of the CNU board of directors. Dittmar cites two reasons for this: First, promoting TOD is "nobody's business"—or, at least, nobody's primary business. Even its biggest promoters, transit agencies, have more pressing issues to deal with. Second and more important, there is not yet a body of knowledge about proper densities and other factors that planners and developers need to build with confidence. "We've had a decade of experimentation, some more successful than others," says Dittmar. "We now have enough on the ground to start to put together data on what works best, so we can create performance standards that you can count on."

Legal Motivations

While transit-oriented development is the most talked-about generator of increased urban density, government actions also come into play. In suburban Seattle, a mixed-use project called Issaquah Highlands is rising without a rail line in sight. There, the incentive for a density that is "not downtown but more than a suburban office park" is a state-mandated "growth boundary," according to CNU cofounder Peter Calthorpe, whose Berkeley, California-based urban design firm Calthorpe Associates master planned the development. Washington is one of several states that have enacted laws restricting the extension of urban infrastructure within such boundaries in an effort to tame sprawl. Issaquah Highlands, a 2,000-acre "new town" 17 miles east of Seattle, sits just inside that boundary. "The developers will tell you that they would never be doing this mix or this density without the boundary," says Calthorpe, author of *The Next American Metropolis.*

Anchored by a major new campus for Microsoft that is just about to break ground, Issaquah Highlands will feature a town center with small stores and 3,300 units of housing ranging from apartments and medium-density "cottages" to large-lot single-family houses—a mix that is rare for a greenfield site so far from a city center. "Because of the growth boundary, high-density mixed-use at the margin is feasible," Calthorpe says.

The current popularity of high-density, mixed-use development represents a cultural shift.

Although Issaquah Highlands is not a transit-oriented development, it does employ a novel strategy for dealing with automobile traffic. A new arterial road that connects the community to Interstate 90 comes directly into the town center, but Calthorpe wanted to avoid having a six-lane thoroughfare invading a pedestrian-oriented area. The solution—which Calthorpe Associates is also employing in other developments—is to turn the road into a "one-way couplet" of parallel streets one block apart. Smaller one-way streets, goes the theory, are less daunting to pedestrians. "We had to convince the highway department that it would work as well as a traditional intersection," says Calthorpe. "We think it will actually work better, because the traffic lights on one-way streets don't require a left-turn phase."

More than Polyzoides, Calthorpe is optimistic about the degree to which developers and residents are coming around to a more urban mind-set. He believes the current popularity of high-density, mixed-use development represents a cultural shift. "All of the smart developers have realized that mixed-use is at the center now and not a niche," says Calthorpe. "People want to live in urban environments. Traditional families make up just 24 percent of households. Ozzie and Harriet are no longer driving the train."

The City of Portland, Oregon, Provides an Example of Successful Smart Growth Policies

Mass Market Retailers

Mass Market Retailers *is the global newspaper for supermarket, drug, and discount chains.*

Set amid the natural beauty of the Pacific Northwest, this city [Portland, Oregon] is devoted to the idea of sustainable growth. Portland's strong planning controls have prevented the city from experiencing the kind of urban sprawl common in most of the country. Statewide land conservation policies adopted in the 1970s under then Gov. Tom McCall required every city to adopt an urban growth boundary. Portland's, adopted in 1979, specifies urban areas where high-density development is allowed and even encouraged from rural areas where rural land use is the priority.

Proponents say the result of all the planning is a more livable city, surrounded by farmland and featuring less traffic and more efficient public transportation than metropolitan areas of similar size. According to some opponents of the planning rules, however, the result has been limited economic growth and higher prices for housing.

A Booming Economy

Right now, though, the local economy is thriving. A development boom is underway in Portland, resulting in new condos springing up in such areas as the Pearl and the South Waterfronts. Formerly run-down properties throughout the city are being revamped or redeveloped, or turned into new stores, row houses and restaurants. There were an estimated 6,600 commercial and residential projects launched in 2006, up from about 5,600 projects in 2002.

And while current Portland Mayor Tom Potter faced budget shortfalls in his first year in office in 2005, this year [2007] he was able to submit a budget with spending increases and a surplus. The local economy is booming and tourism in the city is up, raising city revenues. The local economy is so strong, in fact, that the city felt confident enough earlier this year to lower the taxes on small, local and new businesses. The tax cut approved by the city council in January represents the first time the business tax has been lowered since 1975.

A Green Reputation

Meanwhile the state's image as being at the forefront of a more environmentally conscious approach to growth is now being embraced by many members of the area's business community, which sees sustainability as an economic opportunity. "Economic development in harmony with our planet is not only the right civic thing to do, it's the right business decision," said Pixelworks Inc. chairman Allen Alley, who is also chairman of the business plan's steering committee, at the fifth annual leadership summit on Oregon's economy, which was held in January [2007] at the Oregon Convention Center. "Many of the keys to how this can be accomplished already exist in this state."

Portland city commissioner Randy Leonard has a similar mission. Leonard is pushing to make Portland a regional hub for the production of biodiesel fuel from vegetable crops.

The city certainly has the green reputation to go along with such initiatives. Portland commissioners in March passed a resolution calling for the city to adopt a goal of cutting its oil and natural gas consumption in half [by 2032]. And last year Portland ranked No. 1 among the top 50 U.S. cities in terms of sustainability, according to San Francisco-based SustainLane, an Internet and media company devoted to encouraging consumers, businesses and government. The rankings consider crisis preparedness and coping with natural disaster risk, as well as such local quality-of-life issues as local food availability, tap water quality, air quality, park space end roadway congestion.

"We're definitely proud to be recognized by SustainLane for all the ways Portland's citizens and businesses are working together to create a more sustainable community," said Portland Mayor Potter. "In Portland the local governments are leaders for sustainability but it's really the grassroots actions from the neighborhoods and the businesses that make this a special place. The city is buying renewable power and conserving energy, and so are tens of thousands of residents. The city has a green building policy, but it's the builders and developers and buyers who actually change the market. It's the people who shop at the farmers' markets, the growers who manage their farms sustainably, the folks who choose to bike or take the bus to work—all of those day-to-day decisions that make a huge difference."

Portland also placed third in SustainLane's ranking of cities that use renewable energy. (Oakland, Calif., was first and San Francisco and San Jose tied for second).

The city scores high by other criteria as well. Portland was the third-best place to live in the country, according to the latest edition of *Cities Ranked & Rated*. The city has also kicked off the first stage of a wireless network that is intended to provide free Internet access throughout the city. The plan is for 95% Portland to be covered by mid 2008. If successful, it would make Portland the first city in the country with a free network of this sort.

Smart Growth Solutions Are Better at Slowing Urban Sprawl than Population Control Strategies

Sierra Club

The Sierra Club is a grassroots environmental organization that works to protect wilderness areas and the environment.

Suburban sprawl—defined as irresponsible, often poorly-planned development that destroys green space, increases traffic and air pollution, crowds schools and drives up taxes—is a major concern for Americans across the country. And, increasingly, the impact of population growth on suburban sprawl has become a topic of discussion and debate.

New research confirms that though population growth is rarely its sole cause, it often contributes in a major way to sprawl. This research, conducted by Professor Rolf Pendall of Cornell University also confirms that the importance of population growth as a driver of sprawl varies across the United States: In the West and South it is significant, often a major factor; in the East and Midwest it is a minor and sometimes inconsequential factor.

But the most intriguing aspect of this research is the light it sheds on solutions. Pendall found that smart-growth solutions, which focus on channeling growth into areas with existing infrastructure, were effective at slowing sprawling growth regardless of its cause. Other solutions that focused on curtailing population growth by reducing the density of land use, actually increased the amount of sprawl and failed to reduce population growth, he found.

Sierra Club, "New Research on Population, Suburban Sprawl and Smart Growth," www.sierraclub.org, July 23, 2007. Reproduced from sierraclub.org with permission of the Sierra Club.

Population Growth and Suburban Sprawl: A Complex Relationship

Professor Rolf Pendall of Cornell University analyzed suburban sprawl over the course of the 1980s in 282 metropolitan areas. He found that the population growth variable explains about 31 percent of the growth in land area. They found that even those areas that experienced no population growth increased in urbanized land area by an average of 18 percent.

Our urban areas are expanding at about twice the rate that the population is growing.

This new evidence supports the conclusions of a study by former mayor of Albuquerque and author David Rusk. Rusk studied 213 urbanized areas and found that between 1960 and 1990 population increased from 95 million to 140 million (47 percent) while urbanized land increased from 25,000 square miles to 51,000 square miles (107 percent). This means that density per square mile decreased by 28%.

Data collected by the U.S. Department of Housing and Urban Development for its State of the Cities 2000 report (1994–1997 time period) show a continuation of this trend: Our urban areas are expanding at about twice the rate that the population is growing. It is important to remember that if there are multiple causes of sprawl, then their impact is multiplied together, so that if population increases by 50%, and density decreases by 50%, land consumed will increase not by 100%, but by 300%. So poor land use makes the impact of population growth worse, and vice-versa.

A regional breakdown of Rusk's data shows some significant variations. In some areas of the United States, metropolitan area sprawl is largely a consequence of flight from central cities, but in other parts of the country net population growth is playing a larger role in exacerbating sprawl. Population growth is clearly a bigger factor in the South and the West (particularly along the coasts) than in the Midwest and Northeast. In fact, according to a recent study of 277 metropolitan areas by Janet Rothenberg Pack of the University of Pennsylvania, from 1960–1990 our western cities nearly doubled in population, southern cities increased 70 percent, and cities in the Midwest and the Northeast grew by a more modest 25 percent and 12.5 percent respectively.

Subsidies and Population Growth: The Self-fulfilling Cycle

A growing body of research shows that many communities are subsidizing new development in the form of new roads, water and sewer lines, schools, and emergency services. Communities are also subsidizing growth by offering incentives to new businesses or industries that locate there, often sacrificing tax revenues needed to serve existing residents and businesses.

This issue has arisen recently in Texas, where officials and citizens are debating a proposal to spend $17 billion on water-related infrastructure, like dams and reservoirs, over the next 50 years. This new development is designed to support a projected near-doubling of the state's population. The big question is: Does this kind of infrastructure planning prove to be a self-fulfilling prophecy?

In addition to infrastructure investments, cities, states and communities across America spend billions of dollars to attract corporations to their areas.

There's evidence in the transportation arena that this cycle of subsidies does encourage growth. A recent study prepared for the Brookings Institution found that "changes in metropolitan patterns are induced by highways." And the Maryland Public Interest Research Group found a "magnet effect" as well as a "ripple effect" whereby new highway construction not only attracted new development, but that this effect became more pronounced as distance from an urban area increased. In other words, the further we extend roads and other infrastructure from existing communities, the more this tends to generate sprawl.

In addition to infrastructure investments, cities, states and communities across America spend billions of dollars to attract corporations to their areas. These relocations are often a contributor to sprawl. Greg LeRoy of the Good Jobs First program at the Institute on Taxation and Economic Policy (ITEP) studied this phenomenon in Anoka, a suburb of [the] Minneapolis-St. Paul area. What he found was that 26 of the 29 companies which had relocated (thanks to $7.5 million worth of free land subsidies) came from the "urban core area or closer to it than Anoka." In the process, about 1200 jobs moved away from the central city.

In an earlier study of 550 economic development disclosure subsidies in Minnesota, LeRoy and Tyson Slocum of ITEP found an equally disturbing pattern: Little heed was paid in terms of the kinds of job growth encouraged by $176 million worth of economic incentives. The per-job subsidies were sizable, with "One hundred and twenty-three deals approved at a cost of more than $35,000 per job . . .[and] Thirty-eight deals approved at $100,000 or more per job." What Minnesota jurisdictions received in exchange for these incentives were jobs paying lower wages than normal. In fact, "About two-thirds of the deals were approved despite very low projected wages—20% or more below market levels for their industries. Roughly half the deals report actual wages that low."

This dynamic is similar to what Bruce Katz and Joel Rogers of the Brookings Institution refer to when they talk about "low road" economic strategies for metropolitan areas. And it matters not just for central cities, but for metropolitan regions as a whole. In fact, Katz and Rogers found that, "By the late 1980s, across a very wide range of metropolitan regions, every $1,000 gained or lost in per capita city income was associated with a $690 gain or loss in per capita suburban income. And indeed, recent evidence suggests the urban-suburban economic linkage is getting tighter over time."

Breaking the cycle of subsidies can help us curb suburban sprawl while also restraining population growth.

Katz and Rogers as well as LeRoy highly recommend setting wage floors when writing contracts, grants, or offering subsidies for new businesses. This is crucial and helps to counter the misconception that all job growth is always good. Regions looking out for their long-term economic interests need to hew to a "high road" strategy. This also helps to address the problem of rapid population growth, which is most likely spurred by an anything-goes job growth strategy uninformed by concerns about wage levels.

Subsidies have clearly played a role in encouraging, or at least enabling, sprawling development. But the good news is that breaking the cycle of subsidies can help us curb suburban sprawl while also restraining population growth by tying it to the availability of key resources, like water.

Solutions that Work: Grow Smarter

Professor Rolf Pendall's recent study found that smart-growth tools like Adequate Public Facilities Ordinances (APFOs), which require that infrastructure like roads and sewer lines be fully paid for before new development moves forward, are very effective. His research bears out the effectiveness of a strategy that demands that growth should pay its own way.

Interestingly, Pendall's research has also confirmed the importance of supporting farmers and shoring up the farm economy. He found that "the value of farm products sold per acre of farmland is by far the most important variable related to sprawl versus compactness. Every additional $1000 of productivity in 1982 was associated with about 70 new residents per 100 new urban acres between 1982 and 1992."

Another key smart-growth solution that has proven very effective is the use of greenbelts. Greenbelts create designated growth areas with distinct boundaries and protection for open spaces outside of those boundaries.

Most of these policies also deal with population growth. However, their focus isn't on overall numbers of people, it's on the location of human settlements. More specifically, their general purpose is to channel population growth away from areas that should be off-limits, like floodplains, wetlands, and important habitats.

The state of Oregon is the best example of this policy. Oregon adopted several statewide planning statutes in 1973, including one requiring the adoption of plans which zone for affordable housing within urban growth boundaries and the creation of protective zones outside of them. The plan has meant the protection of 25 million acres' worth of farm and forest lands. It has also allowed Portland's population to grow by 50 percent since the 1970s while its land area increased by a mere 2 percent.

On the opposite side of the growth management spectrum is Atlanta, variously referred to as "Hotlanta" and "Sprawl City" because of its rapid growth. From the mid-80s to the mid-90s, Atlanta grew at about the same rate as Portland (32 percent versus 26 percent). But without strong growth management rules, Atlanta has sprawled rapidly. In fact, during the 1990s, the region doubled in size from 65 miles north to south to a staggering 110 miles. This growth hasn't been evenly distributed. In 1998, growth in Atlanta's suburbs was 100 times the growth in the city.

As Professor Chris Nelson of Georgia Tech found when he compared growth issues in Atlanta and Portland from the mid-80s to the mid-90s, smart growth policies like urban growth boundaries yield plenty of other benefits. Atlanta's property taxes have shot up 22 percent in that period, whereas Portland's dropped 29 percent. Vehicle miles traveled jumped 17 percent in Atlanta but rose a bare 2 percent in Portland. And the extra miles drivers must travel in Atlanta have an impact on air quality: Nelson found that ground-level ozone, measured by number of days with unhealthy concentrations in the ambient air, plummeted in Portland by 86 percent but rose 5 percent in Atlanta.

In addition to cutting the subsidy cycle and using greenbelts to protect our open spaces, the Sierra Club strongly favors other tools which provide an economic disincentive for sprawl, including:

- Location-Efficient Mortgages, which provide better loan terms based on a home's proximity to public transportation or the center of a city;

- Impact fees, which are charged to developers to pay for new infrastructure;

- Split-rate property taxes, which encourage development in existing communities by taxing buildings at a lower rate than land; and

- Cutting subsidies for low-wage industries and by setting specific requirements such as wage floors (LeRoy of ITEP suggests they be set at local market levels) as well as low or no pollution levels.

Tactics that attempt to discourage population growth by reducing density can backfire and lead to more sprawl and more growth.

All of these tools intrinsically deal with population growth by rendering areas, especially environmentally fragile places, off-limits to new development and instead channeling growth into areas that can handle it.

Ineffective and Inequitable Ideas: Reducing Density

Though smart growth solutions have proven effective, tactics that attempt to discourage population growth by reducing density can backfire and lead to more sprawl and more growth.

Professor Pendall surveyed the use of growth management tools by planners and engineers in 159 counties that gained population between 1982 and 1992. He performed a regression analysis on the impact of these tools on sprawl-based land consumption. His findings are striking: Tools aimed specifically at slowing population growth by use of low-density zoning, were actually associated with more sprawl.

In a separate study Pendall highlights another reason to be wary of tools aimed at simply capping growth by reducing density: They can be racially and economically exclusionary, in part because they are invariably implemented only in certain jurisdictions within a metropolitan region. In this article, using a survey of more than 1,000 jurisdictions in the 25 largest U.S. metropolitan areas, Pendall shows that low-density-only zoning excludes blacks and Hispanics by restricting the construction of multifamily and rental housing.

Pendall convincingly sketches out a "chain of exclusion" whereby low-density-only zoning leads to exclusion of racial minorities either directly or by spurring a shift to lower housing production and single-family unit housing, leading to a lower percentage of renters and lower rental affordability. . . .

Sprawl is driven by myopic public policies, irresponsible private practices, outdated cultural norms and population growth. The mix of these factors is different in every metropolitan area, and varies widely from region to region. Poor planning and population growth interact with each and exacerbate their negative impacts. The solutions must, similarly, be crafted on the basis of local circumstances and needs.

Though population is one of the factors that creates sprawl, not all solutions that appear to focus on population actually work. Solutions that focus on low density in particular can backfire. Not only can these "solutions" actually increase the amount of suburban sprawl, but also they are often unfair and exclusionary.

The good news is that smart growth solutions—like cutting the subsidies to both development and job relocation that feed sprawl and using greenbelts to protect fragile areas—can actually restrain population growth while curbing suburban sprawl. In short, whatever the mix of population growth and poor land use practices that cause sprawl in a given region, smart growth solutions are still the most effective and equitable way to combat suburban sprawl.

Smart Growth Works Best When Directed Away from Ecologically Sensitive Areas

Defenders of Wildlife

Defenders of Wildlife is a national, nonprofit membership organization that is dedicated to the conservation of all native species of plants and animals in functioning ecosystems.

Sprawling human settlement—rapidly growing, low density, automobile-dependent communities that consume land beyond the edges of existing towns and cities—typically displace all but the most adaptable species of fish and wildlife. . . .

Sprawl Threatens Wildlife and Habitat

More than one-third of the known species in the United States are considered in danger of extinction. The main threat to these species, and biodiversity in general, is habitat loss and fragmentation. While habitat can be consumed and altered in numerous ways, poorly planned development and unmanaged growth, or sprawl, is one of the major contributors. In a recent California study, sprawl was found to be the leading cause of species imperilment.

> *If the development . . . is forced into areas of special ecological sensitivity, a "smart growth" strategy won't look so smart after all.*

Sprawl, especially through the building of impervious surfaces and roads, destroys and fragments habitat and disrupts ecological processes. Invasive species thrive and pollution increases in these disturbed environments, causing numerous additional problems for species and their habitat.

Defenders of Wildlife, "Habitat Conservation," www.biodiversitypartners.org, 2003. Reproduced by permission.

Sprawl has been devouring land and habitat at an alarming pace. The rate of sprawl in the United States almost quadrupled between 1954 and 1997 and doubled between 1992 and 1997. About 3 million acres (roughly the size of Connecticut) of mainly forestland, pastureland, rangeland, and crop land are converted to urbanized landscapes annually.

Containing Sprawl Is Necessary

Most planners and citizens who are interested in containing sprawl are motivated by reasons unrelated to habitat and ecological issues. They are worried about issues such as traffic, unattractive strips of development, deterioration of downtowns, the high cost of transportation and other infrastructure, loss of open space and disappearing farmland. Even places like Oregon, with a highly acclaimed land use planning system, tend to emphasize land uses directly related to human needs.

Compact development has been a popular solution to contain sprawl and reduce the human footprint on the landscape. By concentrating development in the urban core and developing in dense patterns, growth pressure elsewhere is relieved, and it is assumed that fish and wildlife habitat is less impacted. However, if the development that occurs (in a compact manner or not) is forced into areas of special ecological sensitivity, a "smart growth" strategy won't look so smart after all. Development needs to be steered away from these ecologically sensitive areas in order for biodiversity to thrive and to allow properly functioning ecological and ecosystem processes.

Conservation Efforts Also Needed

Ecological needs are most appropriately addressed at broad scales, like at regional or state levels. At this scale, it may be possible to identify large blocks of relatively undisturbed land that provide good habitat for a broad range of species and allow natural disturbances like floods, fire, and hurricanes to shape the landscapes as they would under more natural conditions. Therefore, an important element of "smart growth" should be to steer compact development away from priority habitats as determined by statewide or regional conservation plans. These broad scaled conservation plans may focus habitat protection efforts on rural areas that aren't under heavy development pressures and where land isn't as expensive. It may be discovered that those places with gentle topography, water, mild climates and other features so attractive to people are also important for wildlife.

In and around developed areas, habitat conservation is more challenging. Blocks of habitat are fragmented into small patches. Streams may flow under streets and buildings. Native vegetation has been replaced with introduced species. Human activities introduce contaminants of all sorts. However, important microhabitats remain and are deserving of protection and special management. Other damaged areas may be suitable for restoration. Strategically conserving remaining undeveloped lands in urbanizing areas may provide important connectivity between surrounding less developed landscapes. Therefore, an effective local conservation strategy will protect habitat remnants in developed areas in addition to large blocks of habitat identified by a broader regional or state level conservation plan.

Conservation Planning at Multiple Scales

The number of conservation strategies in the U.S. that address sprawl and wildlife habitat protection simultaneously is growing. These plans and programs vary in approach and purpose and range from local (i.e., city, township) to multi-state in scale. The most effective plans are integrated and coordinated with biodiversity protection plans at broader scales, such as regional or statewide plans. . . .

An important conservation goal for local jurisdictions should be to direct development away from ecologically sensitive areas and areas that can be restored, which can be identified by regional or state plans or local inventories. Various local planning methods can be used to help achieve this goal, such as creating a local conservation plan or incorporating conservation goals into a comprehensive land use plan.

Smart Growth Is a Threat to the American Dream

Wendell Cox

Wendell Cox is a senior fellow of The Heartland Institute, a nonprofit organization in Chicago, Illinois, that promotes free-market solutions to social and economic problems. Cox is also a consultant to public-policy, planning, and transportation organizations; and a visiting professor at a French national university.

Simply described as the geographical spreading out of urban areas, "urban sprawl" has become the stuff of public policy hysteria. A well-financed movement blames sprawl for everything from a lack of community spirit to obesity. The movement has labeled itself "smart growth," but more descriptive—and more accurate—would be "anti-opportunity." It would force housing prices up, depriving millions of households, disproportionately minority, of home ownership. It would increase commuter travel times and reduce the number of jobs accessible, to the disproportionate harm of lower-income households, especially minorities.

The "smart growth" movement is a serious threat to the American Dream of home ownership, employment, and prosperity. Far more dangerous than black cats, ladders, and Friday the 13th, it jeopardizes the lives of millions of Americans. The 13 myths debunked below explain why.

Myth #1: Smart Growth Does Not Reduce Housing Affordability. Rationing raises prices. Smart growth measures ration land by forcing higher densities through urban growth boundaries, excessive impact fees, down-zoning and other restrictions on development. This drives prices higher, making housing less affordable.

Wendell Cox, "Debunking Friday the 13th: 13 Myths of Urban Sprawl," The Heartland Institute, June 12, 2003. www.heartland.org. Reproduced by permission.

Myth #2: Higher Densities Mean Less Traffic Congestion. National and international evidence clearly shows higher densities increase traffic congestion. Per-capita travel by automobile may decline a bit as densities rise, but not enough to keep traffic from getting a lot worse. Adding more of anything to a constricted space—putting more people into smaller urban areas—increases crowding.

Myth #3: Lower Densities Mean Higher Costs of Government. The smart-growth folks say we can "no longer afford" our low-density lifestyle, claiming higher taxes and fees are caused by lower densities. But the data show lower-density cities have *lower* expenditure levels than higher-density cities. Moreover, cities with newer housing stock (second- and third-ring suburbs) have *lower* public expenditures than central cities and first-ring suburbs.

Myth #4: Higher Densities Mean Less Air Pollution. EPA [Environmental Protection Agency] research concludes air pollution emissions are higher where traffic speeds are slower, and emissions are higher where there is more stop-and-go traffic. Higher densities mean more traffic congestion, which in turn means slower traffic speeds and more stop-and-go travel. More tailpipes do not emit less pollution.

America has become increasingly urban, as rural residents have moved to urban areas, where they have accounted for much of suburban growth.

Myth #5: Central Cities Are Victims of Suburban Growth. America's central cities have lost population, while suburbs have gained. It does not, however, follow that city losses occurred because of suburban growth.

Over the past half-century, America has become increasingly urban, as rural residents have moved to urban areas, where they have accounted for much of suburban growth. And cities have driven away many who would have stayed.

"Cities" are hardly the victims here. City residents are: residents who felt they had no choice but to leave, and even more so those who have no choice but to stay, captive to governments qualifying as third world by their performance.

Myth #6: Rail Transit Reduces Traffic Congestion. There is no evidence—none—that new rail transit has materially reduced traffic congestion in any urban area. Building rail is justified principally by an irresistible urge to spend taxpayers' money. The higher the cost, railvangelists claim, the greater the benefit. Of course, the historic rail systems serving the pre-automobile cores of New York, Chicago, Paris, London, Tokyo, or Hong Kong are essential. But Sioux City, Iowa, is not Hong Kong. Neither, for that matter, is Portland.

Myth #7: Rail Transit Is Needed for "Transportation Choice". From Cincinnati to Austin, transit spending advocates quickly abandon their baseless traffic congestion claims when challenged. They shift to what they call "transportation choice"—the idea that building rail transit provides choices for people. But choices for whom? At most, rail transit serves the small percentage of people who work downtown—the only destination to which transit provides what can be considered automobile-competitive service. To provide genuine transit choice for all would require annual expenditures that rival the gross income of any urban area.

Myth #8: We Can't Build Our Way Out of Congestion. This proceeds from the belief that new roadway capacity creates new traffic (the "induced traffic" effect)—suggesting a corollary that building more maternity wards would increase the birth rate. This leads to a further conclusion that, given enough road capacity, Americans will eventually spend 36 to 72 hours per day behind the wheel. More rational minds at the Federal Highway Administration found little induced traffic effect, and even that withers away when travel time (rather than distance) is considered.

Myth #9: The Jobs-Housing Balance. "Planners," the smart growth movement claim, should design transportation and land use so as to minimize the distance between work and home. This may be the most bankrupt, and surely the most arrogant, of the smart growth myths. Herding cats would have at least as high a probability of success.

Housing and food expenditures are so much lower where densities are lower, *that any transportation cost advantage for higher density areas is more than erased.*

According to Census data, barely 20 percent of households consider proximity to work as the principal reason for selecting their home neighborhood. A jobs-housing balance requires other balances as well—jobs-housing-education, jobs-housing-leisure, etc. Are "planners" really in the best position to decide?

Myth #10: Higher Densities Mean a Lower Cost of Living. Periodically, smart-growth studies emerge claiming household transportation expenditures are higher where densities are lower. But there is more to life than transportation. Housing and food expenditures are so much lower where densities are *lower*, that any transportation cost advantage for higher density areas is more than erased.

Myth #11: Europe Doesn't Sprawl. American urban planners by the thousands have made overseas pilgrimages, frequenting sidewalk cafes across the street from the Louvre in Paris, wondering why Phoenix or Boston looks so different. What they fail to realize is that not even Paris is like Paris.

The few square miles of central Paris in which the myopic rail-bound pilgrims sit is in the middle of 1,000 square miles of urban sprawl. The situation is similar throughout Western Europe, where virtually all growth in urban areas has been suburban growth, and where virtually all major cities have experienced population losses. Urban population densities have fallen faster in Europe and Canada than in the United States.

Myth #12: Urbanization Is Consuming Agricultural Land. Until the Clinton Agriculture Department set them straight, this was one of the principal tenets of the smart-growth movement. In fact, some 400 years after Jamestown, as the Heritage Foundation's Ron Utt always reminds us, only 3 percent of the nation is urbanized: 97 percent of it is rural.

There is less agricultural land in the United States than there used to be, but not because it has been consumed by urbanization. Agriculture has become more productive. Since 1950, agricultural production has doubled, and more farmland than the area of Texas and Oklahoma combined has been returned to emptiness: open space.

Myth #13: Things Are Going Our Way. Anti-sprawl types often project their personal experiences into universal truths.

Transit ridership increases on a minuscule basis are reported as if they represented a major switch in travel behavior; going from 10 riders to 20 represents a touted "100 percent increase." Friends move into chic new urban developments, leading some to claim people "are forsaking suburbs" for the city. Someone should teach these people to use simple reference books, like *The World Almanac*, which can be easily obtained at the nearest big box store.

The Smart Growth/New Urbanism Policies Have Many Problems, Even in Portland, Oregon

Kennedy Smith

Kennedy Smith is a writer for the Daily Journal of Commerce, *the leading source for Oregon's construction-related industries and marketplace.*

In the 1980s, reeling from decades of urban sprawl, the nation's planners entered a new phase of place-making in the form of New Urbanism. The movement favored development with traditional features like parks, trails, mixed-income housing with front porches and backyard garages, multi-use buildings, and living spaces all clustered near commercial service areas. In other words, New Urbanism was meant to create miniature town centers in outlying areas of larger cities.

Just a Theory

But during the last 25 years, the theory of New Urbanism has largely remained just that—a theory. "Portland has aspects of what New Urbanism would like to be," Scott Langley, head of Ashforth Pacific Inc., said Tuesday. "I don't know of any New Urbanism here, but it's more of a journey than getting there. Maybe New Urbanism is an umbrella thought to [be] what Portland is becoming."

In the metropolitan region, most urban planners and developers look to Orenco Station in Hillsboro as the epitome of successful New Urbanism. But that development, hailed as a success story, has its problems, Bruce Wood, developer of

Bridgeport Village, told real estate professionals Wednesday [May 30, 2007] at a forum held by Portland State University. Even on the development's Web site, the builders of the 260-acre Orenco Station, population 2,600, boast it's new housing "that feels like a real community," suggesting that, even though Orenco Station looks like a community and acts like a community, in some ways it truly is not. "The public perspective on Orenco is that it's great, but it's not financially sustainable," Wood said. "The only way to create density out there is to build parking, and that's a challenge. The private sector doesn't want to build it on green spaces."

Another problem with the New Urbanism theory ... is that it hasn't changed much since the 1980s.

The developers of Orenco Station, Wood said, also had the challenge of creating infrastructure where there was none. Building infrastructure will always be a problem, Bruce Warner, executive director of the Portland Development Commission, said Wednesday at the forum, because private developers don't understand the financing structure needed to pay for it. "We use tax increment funding in urban renewal areas, and the private sector doesn't understand what that means," he said. "We need to build infrastructure, but it doesn't add financing until something gets built there."

Other Problems

Cascade Station, in the PDC's Airport Way urban renewal area, was supposed to be Portland Proper's first New Urbanist experiment, with an office and retail park, a 24-screen movie theater, a 1,200-room hotel, small shops, restaurants and eventually residential units planned for its 120 acres. It failed. One of Cascade Station's major selling points was a new MAX light-rail line that would pass by it on the way to Portland International Airport. On Sept. 10, 2001, the airport MAX line opened. The next day's events put Cascade Station on hold, until recently, when the project's entire scope changed to include big-box retailers like Ikea, which will open a store there July 25. What was slated to be Portland's shining example of New Urbanism turned into not much more than another retail hub on the outskirts of town.

Subdivided development areas that had once sprawled are beginning to redevelop around a mix of uses.

Another problem with the New Urbanism theory, Peter Calthorpe, a Berkeley, Calif., architect and planner, told the group Wednesday, is that it hasn't changed much since the 1980s. "New Urbanism has been taken for granted as retro, a throwback," he said. "Adding several layers over the years is how you update New Urbanism."

The way to do that is to combine some of New Urbanism's original principles—diversity of uses and a mix of people—with new ones like conservation, restoration and transportation, Calthorpe said. City Commissioner Sam Adams, the most vocal advocate for a Burnside-Couch streetcar line, suggested planners start thinking about development-oriented transit instead of the traditional transit-oriented development, saying . . . if you build the transportation, businesses will follow. Langley, who moderated the forum, agreed, saying subdivided development areas that had once sprawled are beginning to redevelop around a mix of uses. "It's about adding connectivity," he said. "Wherever there are six lanes of street with one-story buildings, that's a real estate resource."

Population Control Is Essential to Stopping Urban Sprawl

NumbersUSA

NumbersUSA is a nonprofit, nonpartisan, public policy organization that favors an environmentally sustainable and economically just America.

A major controversy in the efforts to halt rural land loss is whether land-use and consumption decisions are the primary engines of urban sprawl, or whether it is the nation's continuing population boom providing most of the power driving the expansion. A *careful analysis* of U.S. Census Bureau and U.S. Department of Agriculture data found that the two sprawl factors share equally in the blame:

1. *Per Capita Sprawl:* About half the sprawl nationwide appears to be related to the land-use and consumption choices that lead to an increase in the average amount of urban land per resident.

2. *Population Growth:* The other half of sprawl is related to the increase in the number of residents.

What Is Sprawl?

Although there are many definitions of sprawl, a central component of most definitions and of most people's understanding of sprawl is this: Sprawl is the spreading out of a city and its suburbs over more and more rural land at the periphery of an urban area. This involves the conversion of open space (rural land) into built-up, developed land over time.

From the standpoint of urban planning institutions, the style of that conversion can sometimes be more important than the amount of the conversion. Organizations whose chief concerns involve urban planning goals may tend to emphasize qualitative attributes of sprawl—such as attractiveness, pedestrian-friendliness and compactness.

But for those who are most concerned about the effect of sprawl on the natural environment and agricultural resources, the more important overall measure of sprawl is the actual amount of land that has been urbanized. Knowing the actual square miles of urban expansion (sprawl) provides a key indicator of the threat to the natural environment, to the nation's agricultural productivity and to the quality of life of people who live in cities and in the small towns and farms that are near cities.

Both the urban planning and environmentalist approaches to sprawl are valid ones for achieving sometimes differing— although not necessarily competing—goals.

Focusing on the Amount of Land Lost

NumbersUSA.com adopts the environmentalist emphasis. It uses the term "sprawl" to refer to the reduction of rural land due to the increase of the total size of the land area of a city and its suburbs over a particular period of time. That definition of sprawl is certainly not the only one. But it is unequalled as a standard quantitative measure of rural urbanization in cities in all regions of the country. Sprawl City uses this definition because it is based on the unrivaled measurements of Urbanized Areas by the U.S. Bureau of Census. No other source so methodically and with such standardization measures the loss of rural land to urbanization.

This measurement by amount closely resembles the most common American understanding of sprawl. For example, if an Urbanized Area covered 10 square miles in 1980 and covered 12 square miles in 1990, it would be common to say that the city and its suburbs over that period of time "sprawled 2 square miles." If 25 square miles of open spaces around a city are urbanized, most Americans would consider that to be 25 square miles of sprawl, regardless of whether it was developed tastefully or not. They might be more offended by the sprawl if it included ugly development than if it was 25 square miles of well-planned sprawl, but the amount of sprawl—and the number of rural acres lost—would be the same. Thus, using this measure, it is possible to have well-planned sprawl or chaotic sprawl, to have high-density or low-density sprawl, to have auto-dependent or mass-transit-oriented sprawl. But regardless of the quality of the sprawl, the amount of sprawl is measured by the square miles of rural land eliminated by urban development.

None of that is to say that the quality of sprawl doesn't affect the amount of sprawl. Generally, well-planned sprawl will result in fewer square miles of rural land being covered by urban development. And environmentalists are interested in the urban planning aspects of anti-sprawl work because they can reduce the amount of energy used by and pollution produced by residents. And better planned sprawl is likely to keep its residents happier and less likely to decide later to move even farther beyond the urban center.

The virtual void of population-stabilization plans ... is related to a belief that population growth can be accommodated without causing sprawl.

Clearly, though, the amount of rural land lost to sprawl is the key issue from an environmentalist and agricultural perspective. The amount of rural land loss and urban expansion also is significant to the quality of life of urban dwellers. The larger an urban area, the more difficult it will be for the average resident to reach the open spaces beyond the urban perimeter; the increase in urban distances can also affect commuting time, mobility and a resident's feeling of being "trapped."

Population Growth Without Sprawl Is Not Practicable

The virtual void of population-stabilization plans within the anti-sprawl programs around the country is related to a belief that population growth can be accommodated without causing sprawl.

Theoretically, that is possible—for awhile: All new residents would have to move into the existing urban area, and none of the previous residents could move to the edge of the city. Such an occurrence over any period of time could happen only through the continual demolition of existing housing to make room for higher-density cluster houses, condominiums or apartment buildings; the demolition of apartment buildings to build higher apartment buildings; higher occupancy rates in existing structures, including some structures not intended for residential use such as garages, and building on any remaining vacant land.

Even if Americans were to accept the escalating governmental regulations that would be required to handle each year's population growth within existing boundaries, such a success would not ease the massive "ecological footprint" on the rural areas of the country.

It is important to recognize that the per-capita land-consumption figure upon which nearly all conventional anti-sprawl efforts focus includes only the land consumed by an average resident inside his/her own Urbanized Area. It does not include all the rural land in other parts of the country that is required to obtain the food, fiber, minerals and energy for that resident, and to dispose of that resident's wastes—termed the ecological footprint of the Area.

A study of sprawl nationwide released in March of 2001 failed to find any American community that has shown an inclination to adopt the regulations and make the personal behavior changes that would counteract the effects of population growth for even a few years, let alone in perpetuity—

which essentially is what would be required if current national population policies stay in place.

Los Angeles is a prime example of the limits to how far Americans will go in packing additional people into their neighborhoods. No city in America may be a better model of the goal of attempting to restrain sprawl by channeling population growth into ever-denser settlements, both in the urban core and throughout the suburbs. Between 1970 and 1990, per capita land consumption fell until the L.A. Urbanized Area was the most densely populated in the country. Many people find this hard to believe because of Manhattan's skyline. But New York's suburbs are only 60% as dense as those of Los Angeles. No other Urbanized Area provided so little land per resident as Los Angeles (0.11 acre). Most American communities have refused to come anywhere near the L.A. densities.

Addressing national policies now destined . . . to expand the current population . . . is essential to stopping sprawl.

Yet despite accepting the densest living conditions in the country, the Los Angeles Area sprawled across another 394 square miles of orchards, farmland, natural habitat and other rural land. The reason? The addition of another 3.1 million residents.

The Necessity of Addressing Population Growth

Addressing national policies now destined—according to the Census Bureau—to expand the current [2007] population of 292 million (up from 203 million in 1970) to more than a half billion (571 million) this century is essential to stopping sprawl. At the same time, cities which value their surrounding rural land and want to stop sprawl will need to address (a) local incentives that entice more people to move into particular cities and (b) state policies that attract residents from other states.

It is difficult, however, to conceive of many cities in America being able to stop their population growth for more than a short period if current demographic trends are allowed to continue and add nearly 300 million people to the nation this century.

Organizations to Contact

The editors have compiled the following list of organizations concerned with the issues debated in this book. The descriptions are derived from materials provided by the organizations. All have publications or information available for interested readers. The list was compiled on the date of publication of the present volume; the information provided here may change. Readers need to remember that many organizations take several weeks or longer to respond to inquiries.

American Farmland Trust (AFT)
1200 Eighteenth St. NW, Suite 800, Washington, DC   20036
phone: 202-331-7300 • fax: 202-659-8339
e-mail: info@farmland.org

The American Farmland Trust (AFT) is a nonprofit membership organization founded in 1980 by a group of farmers and conservationists concerned about the rapid loss of the nation's farmland to development. AFT works with farmers and ranchers, political leaders, and community activists to protect agricultural resources. The group publishes the magazine *American Farmland* and its Web site contains a wealth of information about the tensions between urban sprawl and farmland preservation.

American Planning Association (APA)
1776 Massachusetts Ave. NW, Washington, DC   20036-1904
phone: 202-872-0611 • fax: 202-872-0643
e-mail: CustomerService@planning.org
Web site: www.planning.org

The American Planning Association (APA) is a membership organization for city and regional planners. The group publishes *Planning*, a magazine for planning professionals, and an academic journal, *Journal of the American Planning Association*, each of which contains numerous articles about urban sprawl and related subjects. The APA Web site contains information about Smart Growth research projects and a search of the site produces a list of articles on urban sprawl.

Brookings Institution Metropolitan Policy Program
The Brookings Institution, 1775 Massachusetts Ave. NW
Washington, DC   20036
phone: 202-797-6139 • fax: 202-797-2965
e-mail: metro@brookings.edu
Web site: www.brookings.edu/metro/metro.htm

The Brookings Institution's Metropolitan Policy Program was created in 1996 to provide policymakers with research and policy ideas for improving the health and prosperity of cities and metropolitan areas. A search of this Web site produces numerous articles and reports on the issue of urban sprawl.

Congress for the New Urbanism (CNU)
The Marquette Bldg., 140 S. Dearborn St., Suite 310
Chicago, IL   60603
phone: 312-551-7300 • fax: 312-346-3323
e-mail: info@cnu.org
Web site: www.cnu.org

The Congress for the New Urbanism (CNU) promotes the concept of New Urbanism—walkable, neighborhood-based development—as an alternative to urban sprawl. The CNU Web site lists a number of reports and publications on these issues, as well as links to other groups involved with New Urbanism and other urban sprawl concerns.

National Trust for Historic Preservation
1785 Massachusetts Ave. NW, Washington, DC   20036-2117
phone: 202-588-6000 • fax: 202-588-6038
e-mail: feedback@nthp.org
Web site: www.nationaltrust.org

The National Trust for Historic Preservation is a private, non-profit membership organization dedicated to saving historic places and revitalizing U.S. communities. A search of the group's Web site produces many articles on the subject of urban sprawl and the renewal of cities.

Natural Resources Defense Council

Natural Resources Defense Council, 40 West Twentieth St.
New York, NY   10011
phone: 212-727-2700 • fax: 212-727-1773
e-mail: nrdcinfo@nrdc.org
Web site: www.nrdc.org

The Natural Resources Defense Council (NRDC) is an environmental action and membership organization that seeks to protect the planet's wildlife and wild places and to ensure a safe and healthy environment for all living things. Its Web site contains a Smart Growth page with information about urban sprawl and smart-growth strategies, including numerous articles, reports, and policy papers on these subjects.

The Trust for Public Land (TPL)

116 New Montgomery St., 4th Floor
San Francisco, CA   94105
phone: 415-495-4014 • fax: 415-495-4103
e-mail: info@tpl.org
Web site: www.tpl.org

The Trust for Public Land (TPL) is a national, nonprofit land conservation organization that conserves land for people to enjoy as parks, community gardens, historic sites, rural lands, and other natural places, ensuring livable communities for generations to come. A search of its Web site produces a variety of articles and information about urban sprawl.

Bibliography

Books

William T. Bogart	*Don't Call It Sprawl: Metropolitan Structure in the 21st Century*, Cambridge, UK: Cambridge University Press, 2006.
Robert Bruegmann	*Sprawl: A Compact History*, Chicago: University of Chicago Press, 2005.
Robert Burchell, Anthony Downs, Sahan Mukherji, and Barbara McCann	*Sprawl Costs: Economic Impacts of Unchecked Development*, Washington, DC: Island Press, 2005.
Andres Duany, Elizabeth Plater-Zyberk, and Jeff Speck	*Suburban Nation: The Rise of Sprawl and the Decline of the American Dream*, New York: North Point Press, 2001.
Howard Frumkin, Lawrence Frank, and Richard Jackson	*Urban Sprawl and Public Health: Designing, Planning, and Building for Healthy Communities*, Washington, DC: Island Press, 2004.
David F. Gardner	*Preserving Open Space: A Step-by-Step Guide for Volunteers Seeking to Limit Urban Sprawl*, West Conshohocken, PA: Infinity Press, 2006.
Tristan Gielen	*Coping with Compaction: The Demon of Sprawl*, Auckland, New Zealand: Random House, 2006.

Oliver Gillham and Alex S. MacLean — *The Limitless City: A Primer on the Urban Sprawl Debate*, Washington, DC: Island Press, 2002.

Dolores Hayden and Jim Wark — *A Field Guide to Sprawl*, New York: Norton, 2004.

Joel S. Hirschhorn — *Sprawl Kills—How Blandburbs Steal Your Time, Health and Money*, New York: Sterling & Ross, 2005.

Jane Jacobs — *The Death and Life of Great American Cities*, New York: Vintage, 1992.

J. H. Kunstler — *The Geography of Nowhere: The Rise and Decline of America's Manmade Landscape*, New York: Free Press, 1994.

Dom Nozzi — *Road to Ruin: An Introduction to Sprawl and How to Cure It*, Westport, CT: Praeger, 2003.

Harry W. Richardson and Chang-Hae Bae, eds. — *Urban Sprawl in Western Europe and the United States*, Burlington, VT: Ashgate, 2004.

David C. Soule, ed. — *Urban Sprawl: A Comprehensive Reference Guide*, Westport, CT: Greenwood Press, 2005.

Gregory Squires, ed. — *Urban Sprawl: Causes, Consequences, and Policy Responses*, Washington, DC: Urban Institute, 2002.

Ray Suarez   *The Old Neighborhood: What We Lost
                      in the Great Suburban Migration:
                      1966–1999*, New York: Free Press,
                      1999.

Periodicals

Dan Bryant   "Farms, Urban Sprawl: Which Is
                      Ahead?" *Western Farm Press*, June 16,
                      2001.

Anne Casselman   "Is Urban Sprawl an Urban Myth?"
                      Discover, September 2006.

*Community   "Urban Redesign Won't Make People
Action*   Thin," November 20, 2006.

*Crain's Cleveland   "Foreclosures Sprawl into Suburbs;
Business*   Think It's Just a City, Inner-Ring
                      Problem? Think Again," July 23,
                      2007.

Pat Curry   "Compact Is Cheaper: Researchers
                      Attach a Dollar Cost to Sprawl,"
                      Builder, February 2006.

*Daily Journal of   "Car Crashes, Obesity Connected to
Commerce   Urban Sprawl in Pacific Northwest,"
(Portland)*   June 21, 2006.

Economist (US)   "Urban Sprawl: Not Quite the Mon-
                      ster They Call It," August 21, 1999.

*Environmental   "Sprawl: The New Manifest Destiny?"
Health Perspectives* August 2004. www.ehponline.org/
                      members/2004/112-11/focus.html.

Christina B.
Farnsworth
"Sprawl Stuns!" *Builder*, October 2001.

Rana Foroohar
"Unlikely Boomtowns; The Last Half-Century Was the Age of the Megacity. The Next Will Belong to Their Smaller, Humbler Urban Relations," *Newsweek International*, July 3, 2006.

Phil Hardwick
"Multitude of Factors Contributes to Sprawl," *Mississippi Business Journal*, December 6, 2004.

Marc Hequet
"Bringing Back the Neighborhood," *Time*, December 5, 2005.

Journal Record
"Sprawl Less Harmful than Oklahoma City Leaders Thought," April 18, 2007.

Just-food
"China: Urban Sprawl Driving Retail Boom, Conference Told," June 20, 2007. www.just-food.com/article.aspx?id=98857.

Joel Kotkin
"Building up the Burbs; The Suburbs Are the World's Future Because Most People Love Them, So Why Fight the Sprawl?" *Newsweek International*, July 3, 2006.

Peter Massini — "Wildlife = Quality of Life: The 'Sustainable Communities' Agenda Should Be Promoting Wildlife Habitat as a Positive Component in the Regeneration of Our Urban Areas and as an Integral Feature of the Growth Areas," *Town and Country Planning*, January 2005.

John G. Mitchell — "Urban Sprawl," *National Geographic*, July 2001.

Debnath Mookherjee, Eugene Hoerauf, Stefan Freelan, and Michael McAuley — "Urban Growth and Metropolitan Sprawl in a Small Metropolitan Area," *Focus on Geography*, Winter 2006.

Max Page — "Sprawled Out," *Architecture*, October 2006.

Anna Quindlen — "Put 'Em in a Tree Museum," *Newsweek*, August 23, 2004.

Jacob Sullum — "Thin Population: Urban Sprawl and Obesity," *Reason*, June 2006.

Holtcamp Wender — "Will Urban Sprawl K.O. the Koala?" *National Wildlife*, June–July 2007.

Chris Wolfe — "Steps to Solve L.A.'s Problems with Traffic and Pollution," *Los Angeles Business Journal*, April 2, 2007.

Ralph Zucker — "New Urbanism May Be Answer to Garden State Housing," *Real Estate Weekly*, April 11, 2007.

Index

A

Adams, Sam, 179
Adequate Public Facilities Ordinances (APFOs), 163
Aesthetics, 80–81
Agricultural technology, 112, 117
Air pollution
    automobiles and, 29–31, 79, 87, 108
    is declining, 108
    ozone, 86
    urban sprawl and, 23, 73, 74, 82–89, 173
Alderman, John, 98
Alley, Allen, 157
American dream
    of homeownership, 16–17, 49, 54
    smart growth threatens, 172–176
Animal extinctions, 73, 77
Anoka, MN, 162
Apartments, 57
Areawide sources, of pollution, 87
Arizona, 97–98
Associated Press, 132
Atlanta, GA, 164–165
Aupperle, Dale, 115–116
Automobile, traffic congestion from, 52, 60, 146, 173, 174
Automobiles
    advantages of, 69
    costs of, 80
    dependency on, 29, 46, 103
    in developing world, 103–104
    in Europe, 141–142
    global warming and, 109
    obesity and use of, 29–30
    policies against, 145–146
    pollution from, 29–31, 79, 86, 87, 108
    sedentary lifestyle and, 80
    suburbanization and, 17, 144
    in U.S., 105–106

B

Bakersfield, CA, 82–89
Balaker, Ted, 105
Barba, Jennifer, 85, 86
Barcelona, Spain, 142
Benfield, F. Kaid, 101
Berlin, Cynthia, 33
Big Cypress National Preserve, 94–95
Biodiversity loss, 37, 73–75, 119
Bogota, Colombia, 104
Bonfiglio, Olga, 124
Bowling Alone (Putnam), 31
Branch, Mark Alden, 152
Brazil, 104
Bruegmann, Robert, 49–54, 59, 139, 141–143
Building codes, 82–83
Building costs, 80
Bullard, Robert, 126
Businesses
    incentives for relocation of, 162
    regulations on, 135–137

C

Calthorpe, Peter, 154, 179
Cars. *See* Automobiles
Cascade Station, 178–179

Charlotte, NC, 98

Chicago, 27, 103

China, 50, 103–104, 110, 139

Cincinnati, OH, 71

Cities

declining tax base in, 28–29

depopulation of, 21–22, 121–122, 132–134

expectations about, 59–61

gentrification of, 121

move to, in developing countries, 43–46

overcrowding in, 16–17

small, 34–35

sprawl has impoverished, 124–131

See also Inner cities; specific cities

City schools, 38, 121–122

Civic life, 27

Class bias, 61–65

Clean Air Act, 108

Clean Water Action Council, 76

Cleveland, OH, 71

Climate change. See Global warming

Collier County, FL, 96–97, 100–101

Colombia, 104

Community, loss of, 27, 79

Commute times, 29, 79

Compact development, 169–170

Congress for New Urbanism (CNU), 152–153

Conservation, 169–171

Consumer products, 87

Containment strategies, 23–24, 149–151

See also Smart growth

Corporate relocations, 162

Cost of living, 175

Courrèges, Owen, 112

Cox, Wendell, 144, 172

Cultural elites, 61–64

Curitiba, Brazil, 104

D

Dallas, TX, 152

Defenders of Wildlife, 168

DeGraaf, Don, 25

Density reduction strategies, 166–167

Detroit, MI

decline of, 21, 121–122, 124–128, 133

public transit in, 126, 128, 130–131

racial segregation in, 128–130

Developers

holding responsible, for pollution, 83–86, 89

impact fees on, 165

Developing countries

global warming and, 110

sprawl in, 43–48, 103–104

Dicarlo, Rachel, 49

Dittmar, Hank, 154

Downs, Anthony, 107

E

Economic costs, of urban sprawl, 22, 38, 78–80

Economic development

hostility to, in inner cities, 136–137

in Portland, OR, 157–158

in suburbs, 137–138

Elk Grove, CA, 132

Endangered wildlife, 94–101, 168–169

Energy consumption, 79

Environmental impacts

are less than thought, 105–111

global warming, 75, 102–104, 109–111
habitat destruction, 30–31, 34–35, 37, 73–78, 94–99, 168–169
sprawl has major, 76–81
See also Pollution
Environmental Literacy Council, 21
Environmentalism, 62
Europe
driving habits in, 53, 106, 141–142
public transit in, 106, 141–142
sprawl in, 66, 104, 140–143, 175–176
See also specific cities
Evans, Jonathan, 118
Ewing, Reid, 39–40, 41–42
Expectations, 59–61
Exurbanites, 61–62

F

Farmland
is not being lost, 112–114, 176
loss of, 34–35, 37, 76–77, 181–182
trading out of, 115–117
value of, 163–164
Floods, 37
Florez, Dean, 86
Florida panther, 94–97, 101
Forests, 109
Fresno Growth Alternatives Alliance, 88

G

GI loans, 18
Global warming, 75, 102–104, 109–111
Grady, Stanley, 83, 88

Grasslands, 77
Green Revolution, 112
Greenbelts, 164
Groundwater, 90–92

H

Habitat conservation, 169–171
Habitat destruction, 34–35, 37, 73–78, 94–99, 168–169
Haskell, David, 118–119
Health impact
of air pollution, 86
of sedentary lifestyle, 29–30, 39–42
of urban sprawl, 102
High-density development, public transit and, 107–108
High-rise apartments, 57
Highways, 146–147, 161–162, 174
Hisrich, Matthew, 68
Historic districts, 51
Home ownership, 16–17, 49, 54, 142–143
Homes, growth in size of, 109
Household size, 74
Housing boom, post-WWII, 17–19, 21, 51–52
Housing prices
impact of urban growth boundaries on, 150–151
smart growth and, 172
urban regulations and, 145
Hypertension, 40

I

Impact fees, 165
India, 110
Indirect source rule, 85–86, 89
Industrial parks, 53
Industrial revolution, 16

Infectious disease, 110, 111
Infilling, 99–100
Infrastructure, 38, 78, 161–163, 178
Inner cities
  decline of, 21–22, 121–122, 135–138
  depopulation of, 32–34, 125–126, 173–174
  job loss in, 126, 135–138
  revitalization of, 51
  schools in, 38, 121–122
  sprawl has impoverished, 124–131
See also Cities
Intergovernmental Panel on Climate Change (IPCC), 110
Interstate highway system, 105–106
Invasive species, 168
Issaquah Highlands, WA, 154–155

J

James, Ted, 84, 89
Job growth, 162–163
Job loss, in inner cities, 126, 135–138
Jobs-housing balance, 175
Johnson, Brian, 39, 90
Johnson, Hans, 132–133
Jones, Steve, 128

K

Katz, Bruce, 162–163
Kay, Jane Holtz, 109
Kilpatrick, Kwame, 130
Kotyack, John, 96–97
Kuntsler, James, 26
Kyoto Protocol, 109–110

L

La Crosse, WI, 34–35, 37
Land development, water pollution and, 90–91
Land use policies, 82–83, 88, 145, 154–156
See also Smart growth
Langley, Scott, 177
Lankford, Jill, 25
Lankford, Sam, 25
Leisure opportunities, 28–29
Leitner, Michael, 28
Leitner, Sarah, 28
Lemoore, CA, 88
Leonard, Randy, 157
Leopold, Aldo, 62
LeRoy, Greg, 162
Levitt, William, 18
Levittown, NY, 17–19
Light rail, 104, 152, 174
Location-efficient mortgages, 165
London, 63–64, 140–141, 142
Los Angeles, 36, 60, 122, 184
Low-density zoning, 166–167
Luzier, Michael, 92

M

Malaria, 110, 111
Malson, John, 133–134
Market economy, 137
Maryland, 97
Mass Market Retailers, 156
Mass transit. See Public transit
McCall, Tom, 156
McMansions, 63
Medieval suburbs, 140
Menon, Neha, 43
Metro 2040 Growth Concept, 100
Milan, Italy, 142

Mixed-use development, 88–89, 149, 154–155
Montgomery County, MD, 100
Montreal, Canada, 144–147
Mortgages, location-efficient, 165
Moses, 130
Muir, John, 26, 62
Muniz, Daniel, 135
Mussels, 98

N

Napa County, CA, 150
Naples, FL, 96–97, 101
National Association of Home Builders (NAHB), 92
National Resource Defense Council (NRDC), 97
Natural habitat destruction. *See* Habitat destruction
Neighborhoods, suburban, 55–58
Nelson, Chris, 164
New Orleans, 134
New Urbanism, 26, 49, 152, 177–179
See also Smart growth
New York City, 21, 133
Nickens, Eddie, 94
Noise, 80–81
NumbersUSA, 180

O

Oak barrens, 77
Oak savannas, 77
Obesity, sedentary lifestyle and, 29–30, 39–42, 80
O'Brien, Bill, 130
O'Neill, Terry, 55
One-way streets, 155
Oregon, 164
See also Portland, OR

Orenco Station, 177–178
Orfield, Myron, 28, 126–127
O'Toole, Randal, 41
Otto, Betsy, 90–91, 93
Owls, 97–98
Ozone, 86

P

Pack, Janet Rothenberg, 161
Panther, 94–97, 101
Paris, 142, 175
Parks, 31, 149
Particulate pollution, 87
Pelkey, Neil, 118
Pendall, Rolf, 159, 160, 163–164, 166
Philadelphia, 21, 133
Phoenix, AZ, 97, 134
Piepszowski, Dan, 125, 127, 128, 129
Pine barrens, 77
Pollution
    air, 29–31, 79, 82–89, 108, 173
    from automobiles, 29–31, 79, 86, 87, 108
    charging developers for, 85–86, 89
    from cities, 52
    from consumer products, 87
    particulate, 87
    urban sprawl and, 22–23, 73–74, 82–89
    water, 23, 30–31, 73, 79, 90–99
Polyzoides, Stefanos, 152–153
Pope, Carl, 73
Population control strategies, 159, 180–185
Population growth, 74, 97, 159–163, 164, 180

Portland, OR
    housing prices in, 145, 150–
        151
    public transit in, 104
    smart growth in, 42, 100,
        156–158, 164–165, 177–179
    sprawl in, 36
    traffic congestion in, 146
Post-World War II years, 17–19,
    21, 51–52
Potter, Tom, 157, 158
Property taxes, 80, 165, 173
Public spaces
    loss of, 27
    new approaches to, 27
Public transit
    decreased use of, 106
    in Detroit, 126, 128, 130–131
    development along with, 152–
        154
    in Europe, 106, 141–142
    promotion of, 104, 125–126,
        145–146, 174
    role of, 107–108
    traffic congestion and, 174
Putnam, Robert, 29, 31–32

R

Racial segregation, 122, 125, 128–
    130, 166
Rail transit, 104, 152, 174
Real estate market, impact of ur-
    ban growth boundaries on, 150–
    151
Recreation, 28–29
Regulations
    land use, 82–83, 88, 145, 154–
        156
    on suburbanization, 145
Renewable energy, 158
Reverse commutes, 107

Roads
    capacity of, 174
    highways, 146–147, 161–162,
        174
    need for, 146–147
Rogers, Joel, 162–163
Rome, 50, 139–140
Rural amenities, 113–114
Rural areas
    loss of, 181–182
    move from, in developing
        countries, 43–46
    repopulation of, 61–62
Rusk, David, 160
Ruybczynski, Witold, 139

S

Salmon, 98–99
San Antonio, TX, 136
San Diego, CA, 99
San Francisco, CA, 133
San Joaquin Valley, 86–89
Schools
    inner city, 38, 121–122
    search for better, 133
Seattle, WA, 98–99, 154
Sedentary lifestyle
    automobiles and, 80
    obesity and, 29–30, 39–42, 80
Self-interest, 65
Serra, Ann, 129, 131
Sheehan, Molly O'Meara, 102, 104
Shopping centers, 53
Shorelands, 77–78
Sidewalks, 80
Sierra Club, 35, 68–69, 73, 83, 159
Slocum, Tyson, 162
Small cities, sprawl and, 34–35
Smart growth
    conservation and, 168–171

definition of, 23
effectiveness of, 152–155, 159, 163–167
lack of incentives for, 83
in Portland, 42, 100, 156–158, 164–165, 177–179
problems with, 177–179
as solution, 99–100
standards, 88
strategies of, 149–151
threatens American dream, 172–176
Smith, Adam, 143
Smith, Kennedy, 177
Social capital, loss of, 31–32
Social fragmentation, 79
South, population growth in, 160–161
Space Daily, 118
Sprawl. *See* Urban sprawl
Sprawl (Bruegmann), 49, 139–140
Staley, Samuel R., 68, 105
Strip malls, 53
Suburban development
    in Europe, 66, 104, 140–143, 175–176
    flatness in, 52
    infrastructure needs of, 28, 38
    population growth and, 159–163
    post-WWII, 17–19, 21, 51–52
    subsidies for, 161–163
Suburbs
    are good places to live, 55–58
    contentment with, 59
    critics of, 49
    economic development in, 137–138
    gentrification of, 65
    history of, 139–142
    move to, by wealthy, 107, 127

population growth in, 21–22, 97
    tax burden in, 78
Sullivan, Brian, 135
Sustainable development, in Portland, 157–158

T

Tax base, declining in cities, 28–29
Taxes
    increased, 78
    property, 80, 165, 173
Tax-free exchange, of farmland, 115–116
Technology, agricultural, 112, 117
Thoreau, Henry David, 62
Time costs, 79
Toppenberg, Janet, 132
Toronto, 145
Tourism industry, 81
Tract housing, 18–19
Traffic congestion, 52, 60, 146, 173, 174
Transfer of development rights (TDR), 100
Transit-oriented development (TOD), 152–154, 179
Transportation
    advances in, 17
    costs of, 29, 80, 175
    impact fees, 84
    sprawl and, 125–126
See also Automobiles; Public transit
Tree plantations, 118–119
Tropical rain forests, 74
Twin Cities, 90–91

U

United States
    development in, 108–109
    driving habits in, 105–106
    sprawl in, 103

See also specific cities
Urban development
fitting into existing design, 153–154
in Portland, OR, 156–157
transit-oriented, 152–154, 179
See also Smart growth
Urban growth boundaries (UGBs), 23–24, 99–100, 145, 149–151, 164
Urban renewal, 121
Urban sprawl
benefits of, 59
class-based objections to, 61–65
definitions of, 16, 21, 33–37, 68–69, 180–182
in developing countries, 43–48, 103–104
economic costs of, 22, 38, 78–80
factors contributing to, 16–17, 22, 46–48, 74, 142–143, 160
has impoverished cities, 124–131
history of, 50, 139–142
impact of, 19, 22–23, 25–32, 73, 124–125
myths about, 52–54
pros and cons, 22–23
research findings on, 68–71
small cities and, 34–35
solutions to, 99–100, 159–167, 180–185
strategies to control, 23–24, 149–151
Urbanization, in developing countries, 43–46
U.S. Department of Agriculture (USDA), 113
USA Today, 35, 36

V

Vancouver, BC, 145

W

Wage floors, 163, 165
Walking, 30, 80
Water pollution, 23, 30–31, 73, 79, 90–99
Wealthy
exodus to suburbs by, 107, 127
moving to urban areas, 61–62
remaining in cities, 51–52
Weiser, Matt, 82
Wenzzel, Wayne, 115
West, population growth in, 160–161
Wetlands, 37, 78
Wigley, Tom M.L., 109–110
Wildlife
are not harmed by sprawl, 118–119
impact of sprawl on, 73
threats to, 77–78, 94–101, 168–169
Women, in suburbia, 52–-53
Wood, Bruce, 177–178
Wood burning, 86
World War II, 17
Worldwatch Institute, 102

Y

Young, Coleman, 129

Z

Zoning ordinances, 88–89, 166